FROM PIONEER TO PATRIARCH

From Pioneer to Patriarch

REMINISCENCES OF
LLOYD M. BENTSEN SR., 1893–1989

Edited by Betty Bentsen Winn

Dolph Briscoe Center for American History
Austin, Texas

To Mother and Dad, with love, and to the art of storytelling

© Copyright 2013 by the Estate of Lloyd M. Bentsen Sr.

All rights reserved.
Printed in the United States of America.
First edition, 2013

Requests for permission to reproduce material from this work should be sent to

Office of the Director
Dolph Briscoe Center for American History
2300 Red River St. Stop D1100
University of Texas at Austin
Austin, TX 78712

∞The paper used in this book meets the minimum requirements of ANSI/NISO z39.48-1992 (r1997)(Permanence of Paper).

Library of Congress Control Number: 2012952233

Unless otherwise noted, photos are courtesy of the Bentsen family.

Contents

Foreword	vii
Preface	ix
Introduction	xi
Editor's Introduction	xxi
Pioneer	1
Pilot	47
Patrón	73
Patriarch	133
Appendix	167
Index	169

Foreword

My family's relationship with Lloyd Bentsen Sr. goes back to my grandfather W. R. Montgomery, who was living in the Valley when Mr. Bentsen moved here. My grandfather and Mr. Bentsen were friends and business partners, both involved in the Valley's development. Then my parents—my father, J. C. Looney, and my mother, Margaret Montgomery Looney—had a long relationship with Mr. Bentsen as well. My father was involved in a number of business ventures with Mr. Bentsen and served as his attorney. My father also served as county judge, and, when he retired, Lloyd Bentsen Jr. took over his judgeship, yet another example of our families' shared history.

Because of the close family relationship, I knew "Mr. Lloyd" all of my life. But it was when I came back to the Valley after finishing law school at the University of Texas and began practicing in my family's firm that I got to know him well. Not only was he a client, he was an advisor, a mentor, and a role model, someone I could go talk to about issues after my father passed away. It may seem odd, given the generational gap, but we became close friends. He was a man that was never too busy to take time for a friend, an associate, or even a stranger in need. He set a strong example to follow with his honesty, his fairness, and his work ethic. I watched on more than one occasion multimillion-dollar transactions handled with a handshake. His word was his bond, and I learned from his integrity.

Family was extremely important to Mr. Bentsen. He loved to have his family gathered together, especially for the holidays. And he loved it when he had an audience to share his stories. Those stories are captured here by his daughter, Betty Bentsen Winn, who is the perfect person to write this book. She has that Bentsen charisma—she is charming, gracious, and elegant, as were her mother and father, and she has inherited her father's storytelling ability. These stories capture a lot of his personality and what he went through in his long and eventful life.

Mr. Bentsen was a strong leader for our area, and his life was very important to the region and to the state of Texas. He was a man who, in his prime, was involved in everything going on in the Valley, from banking and real estate, ranching, farming (dry land and irrigated), citrus, sugar cane, insurance, oil and gas, you name it. He was also very generous to the community with his philanthropic efforts and was a stalwart supporter of the Baptist church. He laid the strong foundation that has made the Valley what it is today. When you read these stories I hope you enjoy getting to know my friend Mr. Lloyd.

CULLEN R. LOONEY
EDINBURG, TEXAS
NOVEMBER 2012

Preface

Lloyd M. Bentsen Sr. played a significant role in the history of the Rio Grande Valley and Texas. When his daughter, Betty Bentsen Winn, approached me with this collection of her father's stories, I immediately saw the importance of having them published. Despite his accomplishments as land developer, rancher, and banker, little has been written about him.

There are some very direct connections between the Briscoe Center's holdings and this book. The center is the home of the papers of the late Lloyd Bentsen Jr., the U.S. senator and Secretary of the Treasury. Moreover, this book complements our extensive holdings related to South Texas and the Valley. Lloyd Bentsen Sr. also played a pivotal role in the career of John Nance Garner, whose papers we hold and whose life is documented at our Briscoe-Garner Museum in Uvalde.

In addition to its historic merits, the book's vivid and colorful content makes it a great read. I am impressed with Betty Winn's ability to capture her father's voice. As she told me when she presented the manuscript, "That's how he taught us—he taught us through his stories." The lessons he imparted to his family, and his own take on his life story, provide us with a deeper understanding of the Bentsen family and its patriarch. I'm delighted that the Briscoe Center has now made these fascinating stories available to the reading public.

Don Carleton
Executive Director
Dolph Briscoe Center for American History
J. R. Parten Chair in the Archives of American History

Introduction

By M. M. McAllen Amberson

When the editors of this book asked me to introduce Lloyd M. Bentsen Sr., I thought about the man I knew in the 1970s. Given the isolated venue I lived in, a cattle ranch forty miles north of the Rio Grande, my siblings and I remained hardly aware of anyone outside our family and school, except for regional legends and beloved visitors. We knew about Mr. Lloyd and his vast orchards and farms along the lower Rio Grande. My grandparents and parents spoke of his phenomenal energy and a good number of his kin were friends. On the long drive to school in the mornings, I'd see Mr. Lloyd in his blue sedan moving slowly down the shimmering pavement on his way to see one of his properties. My father used his driving speed as a teaching moment, saying that someday when I operated a moving vehicle, I must keep up with surrounding traffic. On those days, this legend of the lower Rio Grande drove leisurely, but that was not his natural state.

Lloyd Millard Bentsen Sr. was born a man in a hurry on November 24, 1893, in White, Brookings County, South Dakota. His farming parents, Tena and Niels Peter Bentsen, were first-generation Danish immigrants. Their children worked hard and had wild adventures on the plains, capturing and selling untamed horses, trick riding, and learning to become sharpshooters. Although Danish was sung in lullabies, Lloyd's mother Tena made it a point that her children become what she termed "American." They left a Lutheran church they had helped found when the priest insisted on using the Danish language, and helped found a Methodist church where English was spoken. Lloyd was a quick study but received only a fifth-grade education while working in the wheat fields at harvest time; by the age of thirteen, he was working doing the threshing at neighboring farms. Eventually, he took to the rails, traveling with migrants, called hobos, to one whistle stop after another following the crops. He took harvesting jobs along the way, but refused to work for boys' pay, roughly equivalent to three-fourths the wages of a man's earnings. If a man's pay wasn't forthcoming, he would negotiate for his lunch in addition to his salary.[1]

At home in White, Lloyd and his spirited brothers engaged in reckless activities, despite controls set by their strong-willed mother. With rifles, they shot blocks of wood off each other's heads in target practice, accidently discharged shotguns in their farmhouse, and raced motorcycles over the dusty roads of Brookings County. When Lloyd once tested the maximum speed of a Harley Davidson and exceeded the 100-mile-per-hour mark, he collided with a horse and buggy. Bentsen's slim frame tore through the body of the carriage and flew down the road. The girl in the buggy bound the badly injured Bentsen with his belt and passersby took him to the nearest hospital, where he lay in traction for weeks. Later, after discovering that his shattered leg had been shortened in the mishap, he had the leg broken again, refusing sedation because he felt he was gifted with Viking's blood and as a true Norseman could transcend pain. When the leg did not heal, he traveled to the Mayo Brothers Clinic in Rochester, Minnesota, to have a bone graft, a new and experimental approach. During his extended recuperation, he flirted with the nurses and sewed himself a quilt.[2]

With the advent of the United States entry into World War I, Bentsen's passion for aircraft led him to enlist in the army. He eventually entered the Signal Corps, precursor to the Air Force, which took him to training in Minneapolis and Jefferson Barracks, Missouri. In 1917, during a stint at San Antonio's Kelly Field, Bentsen traveled to the Lower Rio Grande Valley in the company of Ray Landry (father of future Dallas Cowboys coach Tom Landry) to go hunting. There he spotted Edna Ruth Colbath, a young Red Cross volunteer, as she passed by on a street in Mission. She was wearing her Red Cross uniform. "She was the prettiest girl I'd ever seen in my life," said Bentsen later. Because Colbath outranked Bentsen, "I saluted her, but she blushed and ducked her head and went on by." He could not forget her, "I've made up my mind that if there's any way to get this girl, I'm going to get her," he told Landry. He contrived a way to meet her by persuading another girl to take him to the Baptist church where Colbath sang in the choir. Despite their mutual attraction, Bentsen returned to his air training and, with a talent for mechanics, he entered flight school at Princeton University for a grueling sixteen-week course, one of only a handful of candidates without a college degree. He passed the intensive training by applying his full attention to study and relying on his buddies for tutoring. Bentsen qualified for his wings at Carlstrom Field, near Fort Myers, Florida. However, the war ended just as he was assigned to the 198th Aero Squadron with scheduled duties in Europe.[3]

In 1918, Bentsen's parents, motivated by land developer John H. Shary and Peter Bentsen's poor health, moved to Mission, Texas. Shary had been in land development and irrigation along the river for several years, especially drawn by the region's growing citrus trade. Peter Bentsen soon became employed with Shary and began a nursery business. Lloyd returned to the Valley in 1920 and persuaded Colbath, whom he called "Dolly," to marry him. While he cherished his beautiful bride, his spirited habits of poker playing and making mischief continued. At a celebration of Armistice Day at a ballpark in Mission, Bentsen and his brothers and comrades caused a commotion in their exuberance. Influenced by whiskey, Bentsen climbed up the speakers' platform and pushed away the presenter. Later that night, he encouraged a sharpshooting friend to blast a liquor bottle out of his hand. When the rifleman missed, Bentsen upped the stakes and dared him to shoot the bottle off his head from two hundred feet. "I heard the shot and shards of glass broke around my head," said Bentsen. At dawn, his friends hauled him home to Dolly, who did not rebuke him. However, in the remorse of a hangover, he vowed to stay sober, a promise he kept to his wife.[4]

He scraped together $384 and bought a new Ford and headed north over the sandy, unpaved roads for a belated honeymoon in San Antonio. Soon, Lloyd and Dolly began a family. Young and enthusiastic, Bentsen and his brothers Elmer and Alton had set to work for John Shary persuading investors to buy land along the lower Rio Grande. They lived as a closely-knit group on a family compound near Mission and socialized mainly within their large and growing family. Lloyd and Dolly had four children: Lloyd Jr., Donald, Kenneth, and Betty.[5]

Soon, Lloyd and Elmer formed their own partnership, purchased land from area ranchers, and campaigned through the Midwest for potential land investors. They capitalized on the infrastructure installed by the previous generation of settlers in the early 1900s, the canal trenchers who brought irrigation water inland from the Rio Grande and railroad developers who scored the terrain to provide for an intensive scale of farming. Candidates would arrive by car or bus as the salesmen would exalt the fertility of the soil and the multiple harvest seasons. The guests stayed at the brothers' clubhouse near Mission or at Delta Lake, north of Elsa, where they were fed abundantly and taken on tours of the area. Often the guests crossed the Rio Grande to the border towns to get a taste of Mexico before returning to decide on their investment. At the clubhouses, Lloyd's children occasionally entertained prospective buyers with piano music, dance performances, or recitations. Bentsen's daughter, Betty Bentsen Winn, recalled, "I think sometimes those poor people signed up just to get us to stop."[6]

The brothers cut furrows along the properties for irrigation and often retained the mineral rights. They planted citrus groves, and, once established, usually seven years later, they sold the orchards as profit-ready farms. Their talent lay in discovering the needs and desires of every buyer, then fitting out a pleasing solution. When the buyer could not pay cash, especially during the 1930s and early 1940s, the Bentsens swapped properties. In this way, the brothers came to own farms, ranches, buildings, restaurants, and other assets around the United States, including a sizeable ranch along the Red River at Clarksville, Texas. Thousands of acres of land began to be bought, sold, and traded. Bentsen covered the country to manage or sell properties taken in trade. When times were tough, he also crossed the Midwest, sometimes with his children in tow, to collect on debts from investors who had not made the move to Texas. Betty, then a girl of eleven, sympathized with her father and offered to help make ends meet. He told her not to worry, "A job does not define a man. We'll make it."[7]

Bentsen, who was brilliant with numbers and finance, used certain methods to increase his profits. In his earliest years in development, he offered workers twice the going rate to clear mesquite and other native brush from land. He paid them in "credit cards" to be redeemed in his commissary, which had the same prices as those in town. Because of the volume of work, he could make the storekeeper's profit, and his workers could take home twice as many groceries and supplies as before.[8] Bentsen credited his first big break to legendary oilman and rancher Tom Slick Sr., who was divesting properties in the late 1920s. He negotiated the purchase of a 40,000-acre tract for seven dollars an acre with Slick retaining the mineral rights. Some land speculators questioned Bentsen's judgment because many areas nearby were selling for as little as three dollars. His instincts proved correct as land values rose precipitously, especially with the close of World War II. By the 1980s, Bentsen estimated the same property at $1,000 per acre.[9]

Bentsen was a talented salesman who understood and loved land. He claimed to buy land that no one else wanted, sometimes for more than others would pay. He convinced land investment firms to buy large blocks, subdivide, and sell the acres at a profit. One Iowa firm bought over 13,000 acres and sold farms to 140 Iowans, who moved to the Valley. Bentsen also established credit at banks and, by leveraging and selling, began to show hefty profit. The Bentsens established the Pride-O-Texas citrus label, contributing considerably to the Valley's $100 million citrus and vegetable production. In 1936, Bentsen invested in a bank. Eventually, he became a principal in the Elsa State Bank and the First National Bank of Mission, later expanding to McAllen, Edinburg, and Brownsville. In January 1944, Bentsen and his brother Elmer donated 586 acres along the Rio Grande to the Texas State Parks Board as a nature preserve, home to a plethora of native and migratory species. In late 1946, he bought the massive ranch Rincón de en Medio, encompassing 146,000 acres. From this parcel, he carved out the Arrowhead Ranch, a mainstay and staple property of the family.[10]

Through the 1930s, many impoverished Valley landowners, victims of the Great Depression, found the Bentsen brothers' land offers a godsend and sold their acreage, which in turn was cleared and sold to new farmers. However, some longtime settlers declined. No matter how much the Bentsens offered for their land, a number refused to sell, including my own family, the McAllens.[11]

In 1955, with his family, Bentsen entered the insurance business with a $7 million investment. The organization, Consolidated American Life

Insurance Company, was based in Houston, and operated by his son Lloyd Jr. He also continued to maintain his interests in farming, ranching, oil and gas production, irrigation, and farming services.[12]

With rising European unrest prior to the outbreak of World War II in 1941, Bentsen immediately expressed his concern for border security. Leaning on his military training, he organized and commanded a Texas defense battalion based in Mission. Lloyd had concerns that Germany might seek access to American territory through Mexico in a time of erratic political theories and subversive activity, and he prepared his battalion and his family for almost any contingency. He warned his children to protect their mother if violence erupted from Mexico into Texas. After the cessation of hostilities, Bentsen served in the Texas State Guard Reserve Corps as a major general in the 12th Regiment appointed in 1956 by then governor Allan Shivers. He was later promoted to brigadier general. The National Guard Association of Texas presented Bentsen with the "Minuteman Award," its highest honor to a citizen soldier.[13] Bentsen was a strong friend to Mexico. His efforts included serving on the nine-member Good Neighbor Commission, an official agency of the State of Texas, founded in 1943 to handle social, cultural, and economic problems of Mexican Americans in Texas and to strengthen political ties between Texas and Mexico and other Latin American nations.

Bentsen credited his success to hard work and his wife, Dolly. The couple rose before five every morning, and Bentsen was often headed to work before six. Dolly held the household together while serving as a gentle anchor for her husband and children. Under their tutelage, the children developed disciplined habits while remaining fiercely devoted to their parents. Lloyd so adored his wife that he swapped properties with at least one artist in order to have her portrait painted.[14]

Bentsen had the reputation of being devoted to his family, but was also rather meticulous and rigid in his business pursuits. He did not counsel his children often, choosing to let them make their own decisions. When asked for his opinion, he was known to say, "Do you want advice or do you want me to agree with you?" Famously circumspect, he told them to be team players, adding, "Let's see if we can be as great as your mother thinks we are." He did advise, however, "Don't hold on to things, hold on to people."

When he played cards with his children, he encouraged them to always play for money, "because you'll really pay attention." This served as a life lesson they remembered. As one observer remarked, any man who achieved as much in life as Bentsen would naturally anger some people along the way. Bentsen did not hesitate to push forward his objectives, even if it caused some controversy. He knew who he was, what he wanted, and worked hard to get it. However, he notably demurred when asked about his children and believed in their autonomy, while he served to protect and provide for them.[15]

When his son Lloyd Bentsen Jr. expressed his intention to go back into national politics in the 1970s, Bentsen was hesitant, but declined comment. Wild and untamed South Texas was changing rapidly to a more populated area, due in no small part to their family. The younger Bentsen, a fiscal conservative and a social moderate, was more liberal in his politics than his father; his philosophies helped him win election as a Hidalgo County judge in 1946 and, two years later, a seat in the United States House of Representatives. Later, after sixteen years in family business in Houston, Lloyd Jr. reentered Texas politics as a Democrat running for a senate seat, upending U.S. Senator Ralph Yarborough in the primary and winning the general election against future president George H. W. Bush. In the 1970 election, Lloyd Jr. was often asked about his father and his conservative beliefs. Lloyd Jr. would joke, "Dad's idea of gun control is a steady hand."[16]

Bentsen sustained his newlywed passion for Dolly throughout their marriage. He credited her for his stability and spoke openly about his admiration of her beauty. Sadly, Dolly died in 1977, but Bentsen continued to be devoted to her. In the run-up to the 1988 presidential election, when Lloyd Jr. ran for vice president under Michael S. Dukakis, Bentsen was often asked about his son's success in politics. Bentsen replied, "My son is a good man. He had a wonderful mother. Let me tell you about my Dolly." During her lifetime, he had portraits painted of her and wrote her loving letters. He wrote poetry to her and, after her death, published a volume of verses devoted to her life and charming character. "Everything I ever did, I did for Dolly. I lived to make her happy. She changed my life completely," Bentsen later said.[17]

In this warts-and-all telling of his life, Bentsen describes the reckless adventures of his youth, his passion for military service, his struggle to educate himself, and his love for his wife and family. He also describes his sometimes-heated confrontations with workers and his vehement struggles to square business dealings, mostly getting others to follow through with their promises. "It's not smart people who make money," he said, "but people who have courage." Across the Rio Grande Valley, he filled in the open spaces with people by bringing otherwise fallow soils into multiple harvests per year. Hidalgo County alone quadrupled in density between 1920 and 1950, numbers only dreamed of before by prior generations. In his lifetime, by Bentsen's own accounting, over 250,000 acres passed through his hands. Never a feeble opponent, he nonetheless did what he could for his fellow man. He was quietly generous in surprising ways to people in the community, while never forgetting to provide for his kin.[18] Even after Dolly's death, Bentsen continued to rise early. He read Bible passages, especially underscoring verses that referred to water, the essential element for farming. He exercised regularly and got out the door early, often before six. Easily recognizable in his blue sedan floating along the South Texas highways, he continued to be passionate about land. On most mornings, he would round up his foremen and go out to look at properties or projects. He was known for saying "everything is for sale, except the family, for the right price." On the foggy morning of January 17, 1989, Bentsen made the fateful decision to pull out in front of oncoming traffic on a Valley highway. One of his ranch foremen witnessed the scene, but could do nothing. By all accounts, the broadsiding quickly brought Bentsen's long, adventurous life to an end.[19] At the age of ninety-five, he died as he lived: moving forward, in a hurry.

---

[1] Joan Sloan Johnson, *The Bentsen Family* (Austin: Privately published, 1985), 25–27, 42; Betty B. Winn, interview, Sept. 4, 2011 (notes in possession of the author).

[2] Winn interview; Johnson, *The Bentsen Family*, 42–46.

[3] Johnson, *The Bentsen Family*, 47–48; Howard Lackman, "Lloyd Millard Bentsen, Sr.," in Ron Tyler, Douglas E. Barnett, Roy R. Barkley, Penelope C. Anderson, and Mark F. Odintz (eds.), *The New Handbook of Texas* (6 vols.; Austin: Texas State Historical Association, 1996), I, 495; Winn interview.

[4] Weldon Hart, "John Harry Shary," in Tyler, et al., *The New Handbook of Texas*, V, 998; *San Antonio Express News*, April 7, 1985.

[5] Johnson, *The Bentsen Family*, 49, 103; *San Antonio Express News*, April 7, 1985.

[6] *San Antonio Express News*, April 7, 1985; Winn interview (quotation); *Daily Review* (Edinburg, Texas), May 12, 1951; Mary Margaret McAllen Amberson, *I Would Rather Sleep in Texas: The History of the Lower Rio Grande and the People of the Santa Anita Land Grant* (Austin: Texas State Historical Association, 2003), 400–403.

[7] *Dallas Morning News*, Sept. 30, 1974; Winn interview (quotation); Calvin Bentsen, interview, Dec. 6, 2011 (notes in possession of the author).

[8] *Dallas Morning News*, Sept. 30, 1974.

[9] Winn interview; *San Antonio Express News*, April 7, 1985.

[10] *Houston Chronicle*, Nov. 21, 1997; *Dallas Morning News*, Sept. 30, 1974; *Daily Review* (Edinburg, Texas), May 18, 1951; Lackman, "Lloyd Millard Bentsen, Sr.," in Tyler, et al., *The New Handbook of Texas*, I, 495.

[11] Amberson, *I Would Rather Sleep in Texas*, 504.

[12] *Dallas Morning News*, Oct. 1, 1974; George Slaughter, "Bentsen, Lloyd Millard, Jr.," <http://www.tshaonline.org/handbook/online/articles/fbeda>, accessed Dec. 26, 2011.

[13] Lackman, "Lloyd Millard Bentsen, Sr.," in Tyler, et al., *The New Handbook of Texas*, I, 495; Winn interview; *The Monitor* (McAllen, Texas), Jan. 18, 1989.

[14] Winn interview.

[15] Lackman, "Lloyd Millard Bentsen, Sr.," in Tyler, et al., *The New Handbook of Texas*, I, 495; Winn interview (quotations); *Dallas Morning News*, Sept. 30, 1974.

[16] *Los Angeles Times*, July 18, 1988 (quotation); George Slaughter, "Bentsen, Lloyd Millard, Jr.," <http://www.tshaonline.org/handbook/online/articles/fbeda>, accessed Dec. 26, 2011.

[17] Winn interview; *San Antonio Express News*, April 7, 1985 (quotation).

[18] Winn interview; *Los Angeles Times*, July 18, 1988 (quotation); David Vigness and Mark Odintz, "Rio Grande Valley," in Tyler, et al., *The New Handbook of Texas*, V, 589; "Seventeenth Census of the United States: 1950, Census by County, Hidalgo County," United States Census Bureau, Washington, D.C. <http://www.census.gov/prod/www/abs/decennial/1950.html>, accessed Jan. 2, 2012.

[19] Winn interview; *Daily Review* (Edinburg, Texas), Jan. 17, 1989; *New York Times*, Jan. 18, 1989.

Editor's Introduction

By Betty Bentsen Winn

Lloyd Bentsen, my father, was a remarkable man. He truly lived the American dream. He was the child of Danish immigrant parents—fine, hardworking, resourceful, and strong people. His formal education was limited, yet he was a consummate reader all his ninety-five years—truly a self-educated man. Dad was a keen observer of life, his fellow man, and his environment. He was a hunter and a conservationist. His sense of humor was keen, and his brown eyes sparkled. Stories of his generosity and his friendships are legion. Great success traveled with him on his adventures and in his business. He was tall and straight and courtly. The Bible he kept beside his bed was well read and underlined. Devotion to his wife, Dolly, and to his family was his life.

This book has its beginnings in my childhood. Ours was a very happy home. I made my appearance in 1931 at McAllen General Hospital and came home to loving parents, three wonderful brothers (Lloyd, Don, and Kenneth), and two good cooks (Lupe and Consuelo).

We were listened to and our opinions were valued as children. Lloyd and I were the readers, Don was the athlete, and Kenneth was the artist. Dinner table conversation was informative and sometimes fierce. When voices rose, Dad would say, "Stop, take five minutes, come back and argue the other side." Mother never entered the fray. We never even knew how she voted. She said that was between her and God. Interestingly enough, the morning after the election, she had always voted for the winner.

Dad was a world-class storyteller. There was such goodness and laughter and history in the stories of his pioneer childhood as well as the loyalty and sheer grit of those early days in South Dakota. And that was just the beginning!

Childhood was busy. Dad was the dealmaker and Mother was the peacemaker (with a great sense of humor). At Sharyland school we could bring our bulldog, Grumpy. My brothers worked at various projects, then enjoyed cooling off by swimming the canals. Dad and Uncle Elmer had a clubhouse where prospective land and citrus grove customers stayed while visiting the Valley. Salesmen would contact bankers, usually in the Midwest, to see if any of their clients were interested in land or citrus groves in the Rio Grande Valley of Texas. The salesmen would drive the prospects down in sedans, usually Chryslers. One salesman was so persuasive he required a bus. There were perhaps twenty bedrooms in the clubhouse with a common dining room and game room.

Consuelo was the cook. Everyone looked forward to dinner. There was no television, so in the evening there were cards, ping-pong, piano playing, and singing. Dad went out two or three times a week when there was a crowd. We went as a family. Heaven help the audience—we were the entertainment. Lloyd would declaim. His favorite was the Gettysburg Address. (He later became a U.S. senator and Secretary of the Treasury.) Don would give a reading. His favorite was Robert Service, especially "The Shooting of Dan McGrew." (He later became a very successful businessman.) Kenneth played the piano. "Somewhere Over the Rainbow" was one of his best. (He later became an award-winning Houston architect.) I would tap dance. I had various routines, à la Shirley Temple. Others would perform. One night I saw a woman sing "Ma, He's Making Eyes at Me," while a Mennonite woman escorted her husband out by the ear. Our Baptist preacher dropped in occasionally. What a scramble! Men playing poker and gin rummy tried to hide their cards. Dad would say, "Leave those cards out. You're doing nothing wrong." Reverend Hickerson would always stay for dinner.

Some of the salesmen exaggerated. Dad would stand in front of the whole crowd and say, "I will not endorse what my salesmen say. Come to me with your questions and I will tell you the truth." One beautiful day I walked into Dad's office. Orange blossom fragrance filled the air. Dad was showing some customers pictures of an orchard after a freeze. The trees looked charred. Later I asked, "Why did you do that?" He said, "I don't want that couple coming in here after a freeze saying 'You never told us.'"

One evening during the prospects' visit we would take them to dinner in Mexico at Sam's in Reynosa. Dad would host the dinner and buy the ladies large bottles of French perfume (Mother's was Shalimar, mine was *L'Heure Bleue*). He did not object to anyone ordering alcohol, but made it clear that he would not pay for it. He explained that he never wanted anyone to claim he had bought them liquor, then sold them land.

When I was a little girl I slept in my parents' room. At night I would hear Dad kneel beside the bed to pray. I would be asleep before he got into bed. One day I asked what he prayed about that took so long. He smiled and said, "When I was a little boy, my mother said, 'Lloyd, do the best work you can every day, then before you go to sleep, turn all your problems over to the Lord—He never sleeps—then pick them up the next morning.'" He grinned, "Sometimes I have a lot to turn over."

December 7, 1941, the world changed and so did our family's world. Lloyd finished law school, took the bar early, and entered the service, later to become an Army Air Corps colonel, surviving missions into Ploesti, a veritable death trap. Don joined the Army Air Corps, later to fly King Cobras in the Aleutians. Kenneth joined the Navy as soon as he was allowed. He was seventeen and became a Naval Air Cadet as the war was ending.

Dad believed strongly in civil defense. He organized and commanded a Texas State Guard battalion in the Valley. He retired in 1963 as lieutenant general of the Texas State Guard.

During World War II, Mother, Lupe, and I packed V boxes for the boys, saved sugar rations, and bought extra sugar across the Rio Grande in Mexico. We schoolchildren were saving our allowances for Defense Stamps, lining up once a week at school to fill our $25 Defense Bond booklets. There were celebrity bond drives and teenage scrap drives. We teenagers would collect scrap iron as we drove through the countryside in pickups. One day I was so convincing about our boys fighting on foreign soil that a woman gave us her cook stove. When we arrived home, proud of our bounty, Dad said, "Betty, where did you get this? It's still warm! You talked that woman out of the only stove she has to cook on." Back it went, but our zeal was undiminished. Soldiers who came to church were always asked home for Sunday dinner. Eighteen of Peter and Tena Bentsen's grandchildren, including spouses, served in World War II, and they all returned safely.

It was the best of both worlds to be a girl in our household. Mother was so pretty and smart and feminine—a delight to emulate. Yet I could ride, shoot, and be given business opportunities like my brothers. One day Dad said he was giving each of us a section of land (640 acres). I was twelve. I told him I appreciated it, but my studies were really important, and I didn't know much about farming. He said, "I know you don't have a lot of time, so I have gotten you a tenant farmer. His name is Mr. Smith. He is a fine farmer but has only one leg." My task was set for the next few days. I read everything I could find about dry land farming. Then I met with Mr. Smith. My suggestions as a new landowner: "I have read that roses and Black Diamond watermelons are bringing a good price. What do you think, Mr. Smith?" "I think that's a good idea, Betty, but I have to support my family on this section of land. How do you feel about hegari?" I answered, relieved, "Really good." Mr. Smith and I had a great crop. It rained at the right time, and Mr. Smith was a fine farmer with a sense of humor. My section was the only one with a little extra—roses and watermelons.

My charming sisters-in-law, B. A., Nell, and Mary, joined the family. My husband, Dan, a patent attorney, joined the fold. My children, Ellen, Dan Jr., and Susie, and grandchildren, Carrie and Will, arrived and brought us joy. My nieces and nephews, Lloyd III, Lan, Tina, Becky, Don Jr., Kathy, Karen, Molly, Betty, Ken Jr., and Will—each brought his or her special gift. We all learned from and loved Dad's stories. My daughter Susan says that her grandfather created a history for our family through his stories. He provided us with a moral compass.

Lloyd Jr. would periodically send writers down to persuade Dad that they could write his life story. Dad's reply would be, "Betty will do it someday." So a few years after he was gone, I began to weave this collection together. At this junction I should say that some of the names have been changed for discretion's sake. There were various sources for this patchwork quilt. There were the stories he had dictated to his secretary, parts of which were more formal-sounding than the vocabulary he used when telling the stories to his family, so I rephrased those in his voice, having heard him tell the stories many times. There were tapes we had cajoled him into making. There was a video made by the Texas Hall of Fame. There were newspaper articles saved by my grandparents and mother. There were letters written by him and to him. There were memories.

When Dad died, I opened his vault at home. Among other treasures were all the letters we children had written through the years as well as telegrams. There was such love of life in his recollections. His telling of them enriched our lives. His children, grandchildren, and great-grandchildren carry Dad's stories in our hearts.

Now you hold the family stories in your hands. You will travel from breaking mustangs to surviving a Harley Davidson accident to flying World War I Jennies to shooting bottles off heads to the most dangerous of all—falling in love. Lloyd Bentsen was daring. Hang on for the ride!

Pioneer

IMAGINE

Some ten years after the Civil War, Dakota was considered Indian Territory. It was not considered prime farming and ranching country by the United States citizen or his country. But for the Indian it was ideal, rich in game of all kinds—buffalo, antelope, and deer. There were fur-bearing animals by the thousands, important for clothing and to barter or trade. Wild turkey, ducks, geese, grouse, prairie chicken, quail, golden plover, and wild pigeon were so numerous that the flocks would cover the sky like a cloud. I've seen prairie chicken flocks so large they would cover a forty-acre field; so dense, you couldn't see a spot of ground.

The government of the United States was anxious to settle up the country. But because there were so many places with better soil, better climate, and fewer Indian problems, the Dakotas were settling up very slowly. In an effort to help settle the territory the government advertised, principally in Northern European countries, that an immigrant could acquire free land, 160 acres—a so called "quarter of a section"—by simply filing on the land, living on it a year, and plowing and putting as much as twenty acres of it in cultivation. Northern Europeans were selected because they were used to the short summer, and long, cold winters they would encounter in the Dakotas.

My grandparents, Anton and Hanne Petersen, in Vennebjerg Parish, Denmark, saw these notices of free land in America and decided to make a new start in a new country "where the land was free and all men were created equal."

My grandfather told me that his family did not own any land in Denmark but was allowed the use of a half acre and all his family could grow on that half acre, in exchange for his working three days a week for the owner of the land.

Anton said he remembered one day while walking into town, he saw a wild goose whose feathers had become frozen to the ice. He caught the goose, killed and dressed it, and sold one-half of it in town for two kroner (about fifty cents). He carried the other half home for Christmas dinner for his family. Small wonder, then, that the 160 acres of land in America that could be their very own appealed mighty strongly to them.

The people came by the thousands from Denmark, Norway, Sweden, Germany, Ireland, England, Finland, Austria, Hungary, Poland, and so many other countries where living conditions were similar. They loved America with a passion for giving them the opportunity to own a piece of land, for being a place where all men had equal opportunity.

In 1877 Anton and Hanne along with their children, my mother Tena (age eight), Laura (age five), and Miller (age two) made the nine-week-long trip across the Atlantic on a cattle boat. Their youngest, Emma, would be born in 1878 in America.

Imagine looking forward to an opportunity to own 160 acres of land for your very own . . .

Imagine a country where you have the right to vote to elect your leaders, to rescind laws you don't like, to pass and make laws that you do like and need . . .

Imagine a country where all men are considered equal and everyone has an equal opportunity—where the leaders selected could be you—where you or yours could aspire to the highest office in the land . . .

Imagine a land where, instead of being ruled by the ruling family, you are a part of the ruling family . . .

Imagine a land where you and your loved ones are free . . .

HARD COUNTRY – GOOD COUNTRY

I was a boy. South Dakota was a vast plain of prairie grass and abundant game. In the summertime the grass would wave like a wheat field. Early in the fall, at the first frost, the grass turned brown, and prairie fires became a real threat to the settlers. I have seen prairie fires sweep the country in a high wind traveling fifteen to twenty miles an hour, with flames three to four feet in the air.

At the end of Indian Summer the settlers would plow large fire blocks around their fields and improvements. Fires could start from natural sources, like lightning, or the sun shining on bright objects like rocks. The fires could sweep across hundreds of miles, burning off hundreds of thousands of acres. Other times these fires were started deliberately by the enemies of the settlers to burn them out. One favorite method was to take a large bundle of hay, tie it into a very compact bundle, soak it in oil, tie it to the tail of a wild animal, and set it on fire. A fox was often used because he had a large bushy tail and could travel far and fast—especially when his tail was on fire! Mama and Pop taught us how to survive a prairie fire. You learned not to run from it. The fire could catch up with you, catch your clothes on fire, and burn you to death. Our folks would build a fire in a protected area where it couldn't get away, then they would teach us to run toward the fire and run through it. We would pick out a point where the flame was the smallest, fill our lungs with air, then run as hard as we could with our faces down. It worked.

Our folks taught us how to handle ourselves in a blizzard, too. It could happen at anytime—without warning—during the winter. If you were lost, you had to drift with the wind until you found heavy timber (very little of that) or a wide crack or a deep depression. You would lie down with your back against the wind, sheltered by the bank of the crack or depression. The snow would drift over you, finally building a little house of snow that would be quite comfortable until the blizzard lost a little of its severity. Many of the early settlers saved their lives doing this.

If you walked against the blizzard, the snow and the warmth of your body would often freeze your eyelashes shut to where you were virtually blind. Body heat would be lost, and you would freeze to death.

Generally, we rode horses to school. The houses were few and far between, and most everyone traveled a few miles to the schoolhouse. Sometimes, when the blizzard was exceedingly bad, two or three would get on the same horse and alternate who rode in front. Most of the time it was the oldest child, bundled up to block the wind. You gave the horse his head. Sometimes the winds were so high we were swept off the horse's back. The leader would take hold of the horse's tail, tie a knot in the tail if he could, and put his arm through the loop formed by the knot. Then each of the other children would take hold of one another, becoming a human chain. So many times the blizzards were so bad you couldn't see a hand in front of you, but the wild mustangs we rode could handle the weather. They would somehow lead us home.

It was hard country. It was good country. Land to claim, opportunity to take. Families were close. Neighbor depended on neighbor. There were those who left, though—a quote from a wagon pulling out:

> 60 miles from water
> 300 miles from wood
> To hell with South Dakota
> We're leaving you for good

I MADE A DEAL – 75 CENTS A DAY (1903)

I once worked for an old fellow by the name of Jack Gallagher. I made a deal with him. Farmers in the area hired hobos for $1 a day and two hobos were supposed to keep up with one binder shucking. I went to Jack Gallagher and I told him, "Mr. Gallagher, I'm going to work for you, but because I'm a boy they pay me 50 cents a day." He said, "Yeah, that's right, and a man $1 a day." I said, "I know it, but you ought to be paid for the amount of work you do." He said, "No, I wouldn't pay a boy more than 50 cents a day no matter how much work you do." I said, "But, Jack, if I can keep up with the binder—then I'm taking the place of two hobos. You ought to pay me $2 'cause that's what it'll cost you for hobos." He said, "No. Tell you what I'll do. You think you can keep up with the binder?" I said, "You bet I can keep up with the binder. I've gotta run but I can do it." He said, "If you can, I'll pay you 75 cents a day. That's more than you're getting now." I said, "You'll pay me 75 cents a day if I can keep up with the binder." He said, "Yes."

He'd go out and hitch up his horses early in the morning. I wouldn't wear a hat, and the hot sun beat down on me. I'd run to this set of windblown bundles and run to the other set of bundles. Jack didn't like it. He was worried about the extra 25 cents that he was paying me. So he decided that he would change horses in the middle of the morning and change horses in the middle of the afternoon. He could do more work that way and keep me from keeping up and save the 25 cents a day. I said, "Look, if you're gonna do that, that's cheating. But if you want to do that, you bring me a lunch in the middle of the morning and a lunch in the middle of the afternoon 'cause I get pretty tired. And I'll keep up." I did, so I was getting 75 cents a day.

BLACK SLEW (1903)

I was nine years old and had a job that paid me 75 cents a day. When I settled up with my employer, I decided that instead of borrowing a gun for the upcoming hunting season, I ought to have a gun of my own. In the Montgomery Ward catalog they were describing a hammerless A. J. Aubrey shotgun with Damascus barrels, which were the latest thing. The price was $12.85. This was a lot of money, but any Westerner had to have his own gun. It had to be high quality, and naturally he would have to pay the price to get it. I sent off for it and couldn't wait until the day the postman delivered it to me. It was the most beautiful gun I think I have ever seen.

Duck and goose hunting in the area was fabulous, and somehow my dad had become acquainted with a man from Chicago by the name of Middleton, who was supposed to be a millionaire—a rare breed in those days. I think Pop had met him when he took a load of cattle to Chicago. Mr. Middleton had asked him about hunting in the Dakotas. After that, each year Mr. Middleton and one or two friends would come by train to White, South Dakota, at the opening of duck season.

Remember, I was nine years old and had my own gun. So, as my dad, Mr. Middleton, and his friends were packing the surrey to go to Oak Lake to shoot ducks the following morning, I came over to my dad and said,

"Pop, you're going hunting, and could I go too?" I could see my dad disliked very much to turn me down, but he thought a minute and then said, "Lloyd, this is a man's party, and you really ought to hunt with other boys." I said, "I wouldn't be in the way. I would take Pedro [my pony] and hunt by myself. You won't have to bother with me. I just want to be there when the season opens." He replied. "Well, on that basis, that's fine. You eat your meals with the rest of us, but you just hunt by yourself." I said, "That's just fine, Pop. You bet!" So when they hitched the horses to the surrey, I put my shotgun in the scabbard, tied it to my shoulder, and put the shells in my saddle bag along with what clothing I might need for hunting, and rode to Oak Lake, ten or eleven miles away.

My dad had made arrangements for us to sleep in the barn of a widow woman by the name of Baggus. She and her husband had settled there from Norway, but shortly afterward her husband had died and now she was running the little farm by herself. She had given my dad permission for him and his guests to sleep in her barn the night before the season opened. This was quite a large barn with a high loft upstairs. The entire barn was built with wooden pegs, no nails whatsoever. Somebody had done a fantastically good job. I went up in the high loft. We all slept between the layers of hay until daybreak. When I could see the sky turning slightly light in the east, I slipped out of the high loft, put on my heavy hunting jacket, filled my pockets with shells, put on mittens and a heavy cap, picked up my shotgun and slipped out of the barn and down to the shore of the lake. It had turned bitter cold overnight. The lake was a solid sheet of ice. There would be no duck hunting until the cold snap ended. If the ice didn't thaw—which was possible—no more duck hunting for the season.

Oak Lake was a rather large lake. On the south side there was a small finger of low land that had originally been a part of the lake, but during a period of drought the lake had receded. This low land would dry up. People who farmed the land adjacent to the south end of the lake had gone in and built a levee across this finger of low land so it could be farmed without danger of flooding until they harvested their crops. It would be protected from a sudden rise of the water in the lake. However, when there was heavy rainfall the water would be trapped south of the levee, making a small slew until the rainwater dried up. This slew was called Black Slew.

Needless to say, I was disappointed—but could not waste the trip. I had to do some hunting anyway. And I was puzzled why the men had overslept. Later I learned they had looked out, seen what had happened, and decided to sleep in. I walked along the shore of the lake hoping a stray duck, fox, muskrat, or something would show up that I could shoot at. After about a mile I came to the levee that separated Oak Lake and Black Slew. As I walked along, I saw some cattle take off on a run. Immediately I heard bedlam on the other side of the levee. It sounded like a duck convention, and all the guests were speakers! For some reason, I laid my gun down on the ground. Lying on my stomach, I eased up quietly to the top of the levee. The sight was unbelievable.

What had happened was that as the water began to freeze in the lake, the ducks had evidently moved southward and when they came to the levee had moved over it into Black Slew. There were actually so many ducks on the water that this water had no frost. It couldn't. There were thousands of ducks jammed together to where it didn't look like another duck could find room. They were crowded up against the levee, which blocked the cold north wind.

I quietly slipped back to my gun. Putting it before me, lying on my stomach, I eased back up where I could again peek over the levee. I had been raised to be a sportsman, and a sportsman never shoots birds on the ground. Prior to buying this new gun, I had been using a single barrel shotgun, and somehow I overlooked the fact that this was a double barrel. I figured I would get one shot and they would all be gone. Because of the cold weather they would not circle back but would head straight south, migrating with the wind. I quietly eased my gun forward, aimed at the center of the slew, not any particular duck, and squeezed off the trigger. Instantly, with the recoil of the gun I thought, "I got 'em all!" They flattened as the shot whistled over their heads. Then the entire lake seemed to take flight.

Thousands of big ducks—greenheads, canvas backs, and more—all fattened on southern Minnesota corn fields and Dakota wheat fields—were in the air in a solid block of ducks. I forgot all about the other barrel. Had I pulled that trigger when the ducks had their wings spread, no telling how many ducks would have fallen. It seemed like they were so thick that every otter in the slew would find a duck. In moments they were gone.

I looked down at the slew. It was quite a sight. Several ducks were dead. Others had broken wings and were trying to fly. I knew I had to get them.

We had been taught that under no circumstances when the wind was cold could we get our clothes wet. If you got your clothes wet in a cold wind in no way could you avoid a cold, and perhaps pneumonia. In those days, pneumonia was much feared, because it was almost certain death. So I did what I had to do. I got behind the levee to break the wind and stripped off all my clothes. I took a heavy stick, broke the ice that was beginning to form around the edge of the slew, and waded in about waist deep after my ducks. As cold as the water was, the air was still colder. When I splashed the water it seemed every drop turned into a bead of ice when it hit my body.

I made the first trip carrying out the dead ducks with my teeth chattering like a trip hammer, and my body shaking like I had St. Vitus's Dance. The second time out, I hit the wounded ducks over the head with my stick. Finally, after chasing them in the water and splashing myself with each duck, I got the rest of the ducks out on land. Then I stripped the water from my body as fast as I could by pressing and sweeping my hands tightly against my skin. In seconds that cold wind evaporated the excess and I was dry enough to put my clothes back on. They were not wet. I had never put clothes on that felt better than those warm, dry clothes! When I was completely dressed—my heavy hunting jacket on and my heavy cap and earflaps over my ears—I was ready to take my ducks back to camp. There were, believe it or not, seventeen fat, heavy ducks that collectively probably weighed as much as I did.

When we went hunting we always carried a roll of twine in our pocket. You never knew when you might need a string or rope. I quickly doubled the twine several times in a loose braid. This made a sling to carry the ducks. Then I made a number of loops, eight on one side and nine on the other, that I could put the ducks heads through—a pretty good sling. I went to lift the ducks up and couldn't get them on my shoulder the way I wanted them. So I lay down on the ground, getting my shoulder under the sling and then got up. I hadn't walked but a few yards when I realized how savagely that string was cutting into my shoulder. So I slipped it off. I took off my hunting jacket, made a pad of it, and put it on my shoulder. Then I put the sling of ducks on the pad and started back to camp. It was probably a mile but I was so proud of my gun and my game. I knew that I would now be recognized as a full-fledged hunter. Because the ducks were so heavy, I would walk a couple hundred yards, drop them off and rest, change the pad to the other shoulder and march on again.

As I came around the bend from behind some trees, I saw I was about a hundred yards from camp, where my dad and his guests had a fire going on the south side of the Baggus barn. They were frying bacon and eggs. Now it seemed a little easier to walk, and I headed for the camp. One of the men looked up, said something to the others, and they all looked. Then they were standing up. As I got closer they saw it was ducks and they were all talking at once. I marched into camp. Everyone, all at once, wanted to know where I got them. Finally I was able to say, "There was pretty good hunting on Black Slew." There was no use advancing the information I had fired only one shot. They all hollered, "Let's get our guns and go down there." I said, "I don't believe there will be any more shooting down there because when the shooting stopped, all the ducks on the lake were heading south."

Mr. Middleton looked at the string of ducks and said, "I believe that's the finest string I have ever seen in my life, and I have just got to take them back to Chicago with me." He said, "Young man, I'll tell you what I am going to do. When I left Chicago day before yesterday, I bought this new L. C. Smith custom-made shotgun, which cost me $650. These ducks carved on the side of the stock are 22-carat gold, and the stock of this gun is the finest imported walnut. Over there is a pair of hip boots, my hunting coat and my hunting jacket, my cap, shotgun shells, and the whole kit and caboodle that cost me $760 total. I'll give you the whole shooting match for that string of ducks."

I could see my dad smiling because of the great fortune that was happening to his young son. It was a lovely gun, but I didn't think the L. C. Smith was any nicer than my $12.85 A. J. Aubrey that I had fallen in love with—it was my first gun, and it had proved to me that it could get a lot of ducks with a single shot. I looked at his equipment, and I looked at my ducks, back and forth, a half dozen times. Everyone was waiting to see what I was going to do. I finally said, "I'm not gonna do it. I'm taking these ducks home to show Mama." Everyone was shocked, including my dad.

Mr. Middleton said, "Kid, I don't blame you a damn bit." I tied them to my saddle, and Pedro and I headed for home.

I showed my ducks to my mother. She said, "Lloyd, let's pick them, and we'll make you a pillow of the feathers." We picked the feathers and stripped the heavy ones. Mama made a pillow tick and put the feathers in it. I always kept this pillow. Many years later, when Dolly and I married, Mama said to Dolly, "Lloyd will tell you the story of his first ducks, but I am going to give you the pillow made of their feathers."

D'ARTAGNAN AT THE COUNTY FAIR (1904)

While I did not go to school much, I always loved to read and would read everything I could find. Books were very scarce then. My favorites were *The Three Musketeers*, *King Arthur and the Knights of the Round Table*, the works of Robert W. Service and of Edgar Allen Poe, and anything that pertained to the days of knights and chivalry.

I was so interested in reading that when I got a book in the long winter evenings, I would lie on the floor by the side of the stove, where it was nice and warm, and read. The other children would go to bed. Finally my mother would finish her housework, and she would say, "Come on, Lloyd, it's time to go to bed." I would say, "Yes, I will, but I want to finish this chapter." Many times when they got up in the morning, I was still reading. Of course, what I would do is doze off for a while, then wake up and read some more. So went the night. My hero was d'Artagnan. He was a green country boy—imaginative, adventuresome, intensely patriotic, and loyal to his friends. He left home at a tender age in homespun clothes, riding a mule, and carrying an old sword given to him by his father. On his way to Paris, he stopped in a tavern for some refreshments. Being so intensely awkward (I thought I could recognize some similarities), d'Artagnan seemed easy prey to the Three Musketeers, who decided to have some fun with the youngster—only to learn to their sorrow, that you don't disturb a sleeping rattlesnake or a hornet's nest. But they did recognize some characteristics and qualities they liked. It wasn't surprising they took him under their wing, so in reality, the records of the Four Musketeers far exceeded the acts and exploits prior to the days of d'Artagnan.

I was reminded of another green country boy, probably ten years old, who left the ranch to go to the county fair to see the sights and to mingle with a large crowd for the first time. His eyes were wide open, and undoubtedly his mouth was too. His boots were scuffed and rough. He wore bib overalls, which were well worn. From the time he first put these overalls on to the day of the county fair he had been growing fast. So there was some distance from the bottom of his overall legs to the ground. While he was going through the pavilion looking at the cattle and the horses and so many wonderful things, three boys approached who were his age or a little older. Their clothes were clean and pressed. He would have dubbed them city slickers, who the country boys didn't like. These three boys decided to have a little fun with the boy who they would dub a hick. After talking to each other about the "g--d--- foreigner" they finally wound up with a statement that they "didn't understand why a certain hick didn't have a party and invite his pant legs down to meet his shoes." That and being referred to as a "g--d--- foreigner" were more than the hick could take. He told them that if the remarks they had been making were addressed to him he'd be glad to step out behind the barn, which they called the pavilion, and discuss the matter further.

The leader of the three made mistake number one when he suggested that he personally would like to go out behind the so-called barn and teach the young hick some manners. The country boy answered, "One or three, up to you." The leader remarked that he would be the teacher and the other two, the spectators. When they got outside, it was only moments until the leader of the gang realized he had made a mistake. He shouldn't have riled this country bumpkin—his fists were hard, he knew how to hit, and he had learned a little about boxing. So the leader decided instead of trying to box, he would try a little rough-and-tumble. That was mistake number two. It was only moments before he was lying on the ground with his neck in the hollow of the hick's left arm and having a tattoo beat on his face. He couldn't get loose. He yelled, "I've had enough," but the boy answered, "I'll let you know when I think you've had enough," and proceeded to carry the education a little further. Some men had gathered around and finally pulled the young country boy off the fellow who was supposed to be doing the teaching. The leader of the gang ran back into the pavilion and found his older brother, who asked, "Good God, what happened to you?" His reply was, "A horse kicked me in the face." His older brother answered, "It looks to me like a whole herd of horses kicked you."

NO PREFERENCE SHOOTING (1904)

In the early days in South Dakota, nearly everyone you met was a hunter and a fisherman, not in the sense of being a sportsman, but almost of necessity. Game was abundant, and there were no game laws. Hardly a day went by that you couldn't shoot something to eat.

One of the most prevalent was the prairie chicken. At times you would see thousands of them in a single flock—they virtually covered the ground and shaded the sun when they took off. But usually they were in coveys of a dozen or so.

Everyone was an excellent shot. In our neighborhood was a bachelor, Ed Stermer, who was considered one of the best. I knew him because his sister had been our schoolteacher when I was ten years old. I was telling her about hunting prairie chickens, cottontail rabbits, and once in a while a jackrabbit—all excellent food—when she said, "Lloyd, I didn't know you were old enough to hunt. Ed, my brother, should take you hunting sometime." I told her, "I'd sure like that." To my surprise, a few days later, Ed Stermer drove into our yard in a horse and buggy. He told me, "Lloyd, I'm goin' huntin' prairie chickens tomorrow. I'll take you along and show you how it's done." I told him in a hurry, "I'd like to go."

The next day I got my favorite pony, Pedro, and rode over to Mr. Stermer's home. He was ready to go. He hitched a horse to a buggy, and we both got in. Because I was such a kid, he cautioned me never to have a loaded gun in the wagon and to never load it until I got out of the buggy and was standing on the ground—the same instructions I had had from my dad and other older hunters hundreds of times.

Mr. Stermer drove down a boundary line between two fields. The grain had been cut on each side of this boundary, but the boundary did have some growth that left pretty good cover. We had only driven about two hundred yards when two prairie chickens flew up, traveled about thirty yards and lit in the same boundary. He said, "Now, Lloyd, we'll tie up the horse here. We can walk down this boundary and flush those two prairie chickens. I'll wait and give you the first shot. Take your time. See if you can't get a hit with your first shot." We walked along the boundary for a few yards. Evidently after the prairie chickens had landed they had walked toward us rather than away, or else there were two others. I don't think the next two that flew up were the same ones that we had seen. Anyway, they flew out of the boundary and made a swing to the right. The gun I had was a double-barrel shotgun. I put the gun to my shoulder, squeezed off two shots, and two very, very dead prairie chickens lay on the ground.

Mr. Stermer looked at me in disbelief, and said, "I didn't even have my gun up. From here on it's every man for himself. You don't need any preference shooting."

We had a great afternoon, and for many years after that Mr. Stermer and I hunted together.

FOUR PINE BOXES (1905)

When my dad and mother settled in the Dakota Territory, they settled on a homestead that adjoined that of my mother's parents. About the time I was born, my mother's father died. He was buried on a corner of the homestead, where my grandmother always kept fresh flowers on the graves and made sure the grass was mowed in the summertime.

A few years later, some Indian Territory was opened up to settlement about a hundred miles farther north of these homesteads. My mother's brother, Miller Petersen, moved to the new Indian Territory. We called him Uncle Mil. He was known as the most successful man in the area, having accumulated a lot of land, several banks, and considerable property.

All travel at that time was by horse and buggy. Even though Uncle Mil was only a hundred miles from our home, it would usually be a couple of years between visits. Usually it was Uncle Mil who came to visit us and his widowed mother, my grandmother. On one of these trips, he talked my grandmother into disposing of their homestead and getting a new homestead in the Indian Territory where he lived. This was finally accomplished. They left in a wagon with four horses, two hitched to the wagon and leading two. They could change now and then and make better time. My grandmother got a commitment from everyone that those members of the family buried in the cemetery, including my grandfather, would be moved to her new homestead a hundred miles away.

Several weeks after she had left, a man arrived with a wagon and a team of horses. He had come to move the graves. After a couple of days of digging, there were finally four pine boxes loaded on the wagon. It was late in the evening. He was going to stay overnight and get an early start in the morning to head back to the Indian Territory.

There were four of us boys, three brothers and one unruly cousin named Magnus. He had been sent over by his father with a promise from my dad that he would straighten him out. (His own father's health was failing.) Anyway, we got to wondering what these people would look like who had been dug up, still in those pine boxes. We knew, of course, that if our folks had any idea what we were thinking about, we would be severely punished.

We waited until everything was pitch dark, slipped out of the house, and climbed up on the wagon. We had a box of red-head matches and a heavy screwdriver. We pried the lid of the first box open. In the eerie light from the matches, we saw the corpse of the first man. It looked pretty bad, but what concerned us most was that we could not understand why they had not shaved him before he was buried so he would look good at the funeral. I was told later, and do not know whether it is true or not, that after death the hair continues to grow. This seemed to be true.

Needless to say, we didn't open the rest of the boxes. The next morning they were on their way to the Indian Territory. There would be a new family cemetery located on the new homestead where my grandmother could place flowers on the graves every day and make sure the grass was mowed in the summertime.

"THERE'S A HOLE IN HELL!" (1905)

Uncle Mil owned the first threshing machine I had ever seen. It was a massive steam engine with a big flywheel and it carried a tender back of the engine. This tender had wood or coal in it along with several barrels of water. When the rig was working or moving, there was a tank leading from the barrels that continually supplied water to the tender so that it could supply power for the steam engine. Next to the tender was the separator that actually threshed the grain. Following the separator was the sleeping car. The men actually lived in this sleeping car with eating quarters in one end and trundle beds on either side of the other end. This could be moved from place to place and do your threshing for you.

I had another uncle who had a home about fifteen miles from my Uncle Mil's homestead. He was down on what was called the flatland. Uncle Mil was in the hill country. I heard a conversation between Uncle Mil and Uncle John, "Miller, I have a hundred acres of wheat that would make thirty bushels to the acre, but I can't find a threshing outfit to thresh it. I don't make money taking it by wagon and hauling it up into the hills to be threshed." Uncle Mil suggested, "I might pull my threshing rig down to the flatland and thresh the silage for you." They finally decided that was the best solution.

Between the hill country and the flatland there was a range of hills. Between these hills were deep ravines called, at that time, coolies. These coolies were crossed over by wooden bridges. There was a lot of discussion about which road my uncles and the crew could take and whether these wooden bridges would carry the weight of the threshing machine. Finally, Uncle Mil said, "I will work it out."

So the next morning Uncle Mil fired up the steam engine, hooked the tender, separator, and sleeping car behind it, and headed toward the flatland over the narrow, winding country roads. These steam engines moved along about three miles per hour, at best. After traveling several hours, they reached the bridge that they were all worried about. My Uncle Mil examined the timbers under the bridge and was sure they would carry the machine. But as he slowly moved the ponderous engine out onto the bridge ten or twelve feet, he heard some cracking of timbers that worried him. He stopped the engine by taking it out of gear, set the brake, and got out to take another look. He decided it was questionable if they could get across or not, but it was absolutely out of the question to attempt to back up with high dirt banks on each side of the road and all that equipment behind the engine. So he finally decided there was no choice. He couldn't block the road; neither could he go back.

So he got a piece of rope, got up on the engine and tied the steering wheel so that it had to go straight. He set the throttle just barely open so that the engine would slowly creep across the bridge. Then he put it in gear, jumped down off the engine and ran across to the other side of the coolie where the entire crew was standing and waiting.

The steam engine moved out toward the center of the bridge. The back wheels finally came onto the wooden bridge so that all of the engine was on the bridge. The bridge began to shake. By the time the engine reached the center of the bridge, the tender was on the bridge with the separator and sleeping car close behind.

There was a tremendous crash! The steam engine, with all the other vehicles behind it, headed for the bottom of the coolie—thirty feet down. When the steam engine reached the bottom, the boiler burst and sent steam shooting into the air. The tender, separator and sleeping car piled down on top of the engine, which by now was on fire. The entire bridge was a raging fire! Everyone was dazed. Uncle Mil said, "Holy Linkabaan!" [My mother told me that was Danish for Holy Mother, but I don't know if that is correct.] "There's a hole in Hell!"

Needless to say, my Uncle Mil was out of the threshing business and my Uncle John bought some cows and fed up his grain.

A GAME CALLED FOOTBALL (1906)

In the wintertime when the work on the farms and ranches was not so much of a rush, we youngsters usually spent three to four months in school.

My dad had read in the newspaper about a game called football. I was probably twelve years old, and what impressed me was that my dad said there were no holds barred. You could tackle the other guy, knock him out of the way, knock him down, and do whatever you could to win the game. He thought that might be great sport. I certainly did, too, because I grew up where little kids liked to play pretty rough and tumble.

Pop said, "Lloyd, if you want to play the game I can make the football." I answered, "Sure, Pop, I'd like that."

He took the tops of old rubber boots. He ripped the leg of each boot along one side so that it would lay flat. Then he drew the pattern from the newspaper on the two boot tops. Pop took a needle and buckskin, we called it whang leather, and began to sew the two pieces together. When he had sewn all the seams about halfway up on the football, he took some ground oats, very lightweight, and filled the inside of the football. He used a hammer handle to pack the ground oats in the ball very tight. He would sew two or three inches more on the seams, then pack in more ground oats. This went on until there was only a small opening in the end of the football. At that point he packed in all the ground oats that he needed and finished the football. It was not as good as one filled with air, but since it was the only football I had ever seen, or anyone else in that country had ever seen, it looked like a pretty good football.

We rode our horses to school as usual the following morning, and I took my football. Remember we went to school only when we weren't needed on the farm or ranch. In our frontier school one teacher taught all grades and all subjects. Boys were from six years old to twenty. The twenty-year-olds were trying to graduate from the eighth grade. One of the local young men had spent two years in a high school in a town nearby. Assuming this qualified him, he applied to teach in our school. The school board hired him.

We called ourselves the Little Kids and so did the bigger boys. They called themselves the Big Boys. We had our playground on one side of the schoolhouse, and the Big Boys had their playground on the other side. So I took the Little Kids to our side of the schoolhouse and showed them my football. They wanted to know how we played the game. I told them, "You lay the football between two goal lines about one hundred feet apart. Then we wait 'til the referee yells GO and we run for the football. It's okay to hit, bite, kick and tackle—anything to win—everything's allowed. The team that carries the football across the goal line wins."

As I understood it, each team had to have a captain. I would be the captain of the team I had chosen, and the other team would select their own captain. I thought I had a right to the position of captain because I owned the football. We tried it. It was rough, tough, and hilarious. We tried it again and again, screaming like Apache Indians but having a great time—with loose teeth and black eyes. It was rough and tumble, but we liked it.

The Big Boys heard the commotion on our side of the schoolhouse and came over to see what it was all about. I, being the authority on football, explained all the details to them. They decided they would like to play football. They asked us to select our twelve toughest boys and they would choose a dozen. We would have a game after school was let out that afternoon. We knew they were bigger than we were, but we thought we had had a little experience. So it would be fun to see what we could do with the Big Boys. We agreed to come over to their side of the schoolhouse, and we marked off the goal lines. Then they told us that the schoolteacher would be the referee. He was their chum—a couple of years before he had gone to school with them. We didn't think that was quite fair, but we had no other choice. About the time we lined up to play, they told us we were playing for my football. There it was—lying out in the middle between the goal lines.

I asked for a five-minute recess and told my team to come to the other side of the schoolhouse. They asked, "What we gonna do?" I said, "I'm not givin' up my football." They whispered, "But the teacher has sided in with them and told 'em we're playing for the football. You say you're not gonna let 'em get it, but what're we gonna do?" I looked around. This was a country that had a lot of rocks in it. When the schoolhouse was built, a load of rocks had been brought into the schoolyard for the foundation. Some of that load still lay in a pile in back of the schoolhouse.

In those days, because of the bitter cold, all the children wore what we called a stocking cap. It was a knit cap with a long tassel hanging down your back. It was left long so that in the wintertime it could be doubled and pulled over your head and neck. I looked at that pile of rocks. I went over and picked up a rock about the size of a turkey egg and said, "Let's all put a rock in our stocking cap. It's no holds barred, so you can do anything you want to. When the schoolteacher says GO, we will all run together. Then you grab your stocking cap off your head—swing it around as far as you can. Hit 'em hard with it if you can. We'll grab the football and carry it across the goal."

Everyone thought that might work, so we all marched over together— our stocking caps loaded with rocks on our heads with the tassels hanging down our backs. We lined up instantly. The Big Boys lined up. Our teacher shouted GO.

We were probably responsible for the word missile coming into prominent use. We swung those stocking caps and tassels over our heads, and you could hear the thud when rocks came in contact with someone's head. Shortly, there were a lot of bloody skulls, and all of a sudden a lot of Big Boys were lying on the ground.

We never stopped. We grabbed my football, crossed the goal line, went back to our side of the schoolhouse on a dead run, jumped on our horses, and headed for home. We knew what we had bargained for if they caught us.

I told my dad what had happened. He said, "You boys were right in trying to protect your property, which you had a right to do." We all felt better about it.

The next morning as we went to school, we were happy to see our fathers and mothers coming along with the Little Kids. We were also glad to see that all the Big Boys had their fathers and mothers along. You have never seen so many black eyes, split lips, and broken teeth as there were that morning—and a lot of black and blue spots on our hands as well as our faces. Immediately there was an argument between the parents of the Big Boys and the parents of the Little Kids. The Big Boys' fathers and mothers wanted the Little Kids punished for using a weapon not for that use in that area. The fathers and mothers of the Little Kids wanted the Big Boys punished because the Little Kids had only tried to protect their own property. Tempers flared when fathers threatened to whip other men's boys. It looked like another battle was coming.

Cooler heads decided that it was about time to get the land ready for spring planting. They all realized that if the Little Kids went back to school they could get a tremendous beating. So school closed early that year. The fathers took the boys home and let them expend their energy getting the land ready for planting.

After all, we could all read and write.

EXPLODING .22 SHORTS (1907)

I remember that little schoolhouse where we and all the neighboring children went to school. One schoolteacher taught all grades from the first through the eighth grade, usually it was reading, writing, arithmetic, and history. Generally there were from twenty to thirty pupils, and since children went to school when there was the least work on the farms and ranches, a school year was for all practical purposes about four months long for the average child. This was cold country, and children bundled up with heavy, warm clothing. We rode horseback to school, but those that were within a couple of miles usually walked.

Our school was a one-room building. It was heated by a pot-bellied stove. My brother, Elmer, had bought a little short-barrel .22-caliber pistol along with a box of what were known as .22-shorts. The teacher would have the boys in the school fill the pot-bellied stove with wood, put a little kerosene on it, and light the fire to warm the building.

One morning it was Elmer's and my turn to fill the stove. I took a dozen of Elmer's .22-short shells and put them in the stove along with the wood. Things had settled down nicely in the schoolroom, and, as the stove heated up to cherry red, there was a sudden explosion, with dust and ashes flying from the stove. Everyone except Elmer and me was startled. Immediately thereafter, there was a second, third, and fourth explosion. The teacher called the class to order and marched us all out of the building. The rest of the shells went off in a matter of minutes. After a bit of silence, the teacher realized the danger was over and told the children to go back in and take their seats. Elmer and I were, of course, suspected. She asked, "What did you boys put in the stove along with the wood?" My dad and mother believed in strict honesty and were pretty severe in our home. I might evade a question, but I wouldn't lie. So, under pressure, I finally had to admit that we had put the shells in for a prank. The teacher became very excited. She said, "Those were loaded shells. The bullets might have hit somebody." We explained that we had tried it in campfires and that the little cartridges just exploded harmlessly. We thought we would have the same results in the stove but, confined as they were, they had been much more impressive.

We each had to stay a half hour after school for a week. With the promise that we would never do it again, we finally paid our debt satisfactorily.

A SHARP CRACK (1907)

One spring day in that little one-room schoolhouse my brother Elmer, age eleven, was sitting at his desk. Everything was quiet. The children were studying.

There was a sharp crack. Everyone looked up. The teacher asked, "Who did that?" Everybody shook their heads and things quieted down. About an hour later, again, a sharp crack. The teacher tried to pinpoint where it was coming from by questioning various children. But the guilty party was getting by with the disturbances so he repeated it two or three times during the day. The teacher was becoming very irritated, but the children were enjoying it.

The next morning when Elmer's class was called on to recite, he still had his little short-barrel .22-caliber pistol in his pocket. He knew it was empty. When everything quieted down he dropped his hand in his pocket. He decided to crack the pistol again. But this time when he pulled the trigger, there was a shell in the pistol. Instead of getting a crack there was a tremendous explosion! No problem finding the guilty party now! As Elmer squeezed the trigger, the bullet followed the inside of his pant leg down along the side of his leg and went through the sole of his shoe.

Elmer knew he had shot himself! He left the class with a frown. Out he went through the door of the schoolhouse on a dead run to the back of the school building where his horse was tied. I thought he had shot himself! Out I went after him. I caught up with him and made him drop his trousers. The bullet had barely grazed his leg, but on the inside of his right leg was a black powder burn. The burning shell had left a streak all the way down his leg.

He jumped on his horse and headed for home as fast as he could ride. I went back in the schoolhouse where the teacher and about half the children remained. I explained to the teacher what had happened. She laid down some strict rules that no more pistols would be allowed on the school grounds. I also believe that Elmer was sold on the idea of not snapping a pistol in his pocket, loaded or not.

BREAKING WILD MUSTANGS (1907)

When I was thirteen years old I was following the harvest through Dakota, Nebraska, Montana, Wyoming, and all around the country. We traveled like the migrants do today, but we called them hobos. We followed the harvest and worked like the devil. Then when we got a little older we caught wild mustangs. In those days, there were mustangs running all over the prairies of South Dakota and North Dakota. Every once in a while (of course, no telephone or radio) there would be a piece in the paper that in such and such a canyon in the Badlands of the Black

Hills there were maybe three thousand mustangs. You could buy the wild horses for $3 a head. You would go in there and rope them up in the dead end canyon. You would rope up three and three and three and tie them together with a little rope between them and a loop around their heads. They wouldn't go anywhere because they had never had a rope around their necks. They could eat and graze.

Two cowboys could ride, one on each side of these herds of three and three and three. We could drive them all day long and at night we would lie down on the prairie and sleep while the horses grazed. We would take them home and we boys would break these horses to use on the farm. If we had a surplus, which we always tried to have, we broke them and sold them for $15 apiece. We bought them for $3 and sold them for $15—$12 was lots of money in those days.

When we had company we would take the wild horses, fresh wild, out of the corral. We would break them, but you lost a lot of skin and broke a few bones. When there wasn't any company, it was a different story. We would choose a piece of land that was plowed real deep. We would drive a post in the center and put a swivel on that so they wouldn't get a knot on the rope. We would get that horse tied to the end of the rope onto that swivel. We would run him in circles around that pen in that deep plowed field till he was covered with lather and tired. Then we would put a saddle on him and climb up. That's the way we broke them when no one was watching.

CAN 'TIL CAN'T (1907)

In the Dakota Territory in the early days, practically all the settlers were immigrants. It was a hard country with a short growing season, so everyone in the family worked. This work started about as soon as you learned to walk. Each of the young boys vied with the others to see who could do the most work and the best job. It was not unusual for a boy twelve or thirteen years old to be doing a man's work.

Ordinarily no one had any money, so at threshing time neighbors came to help you. Man-hours were kept track of. Then when they did their threshing, you would return your neighbor's work, matching the man-hours they were entitled to. If there was any difference, it would be settled at the end of the season, based on a dollar a day for a man and a dollar a day for a team of horses and wagon. A boy under fifteen got fifty cents a day, even if he was doing a man's work.

At this particular season there was an abundant crop. When obtainable, extra help was hired for a few days. This help would usually follow the harvest and live in the stockyards. The farmers and ranchers would go to the stockyards to pick up extra laborers, again at a dollar a day. Most of these men were good, honest workers. They would give you a full day's work. Can 'til can't. It meant from the time you could see to when you couldn't see was a full day.

But some of the men were troublemakers. They had formed an organization called the IWW. I learned months later this IWW meant Industrial Workers of the World. In some cases these men who claimed to belong to the IWW didn't intend to work. They intended to shake the immigrants down for whatever they could get out of them.

We heard of a neighbor's unfortunate experience with two men who told the farmer they would shock his grain for $1.50 a day. The farmer said, "Nope, the going rate's $1. That's all I'm gonna pay."

He left them in the field to shock that particular field because he was moving his binder to another field to keep cutting. That evening when the men asked for their pay, the farmer went to see if they had done their job.

Their job was to do what we called "shocking the grain." It simply meant to take the bundles of grain and set them up so the heads of the grain were up and the butt was on the ground with eight or nine bundles to a shock.

When the owner got to the field, he saw these men had shocked all the grain head down. This was not good because the damp ground would sprout the grain. The entire crop would be lost. He told them he wouldn't pay for the job until they did it right. They knew better, but they were looking for trouble. They refused to reshock the grain. He refused to pay them.

The following night, while he was asleep, some commotion woke him up. His barn was on fire! The men were gone.

DAYLIGHT THROUGH THE BELLY (1907)

Trouble came to our farm when my dad unknowingly hired a troublemaker as extra day help. Immediately, the man got a team of horses and what we called a bundle wagon. He drove out in the center of the field and sat down. He knew sooner or later the owner would come to ask what the trouble was because this man was supposed to be working.

My dad went into the field where this man was. He told Dad, "I'll work for $1.50, but not $1." My dad told him that a dollar was the going rate and that was all he would pay. The man said, "I won't work, and you won't get back the horses and wagon. It's $1.50!" Dad came into the house, and I heard him tell Mom what had happened. Ordinarily, my dad would have dragged the guy off the wagon, beaten the daylights out of him, and fired him. But he had heard about the fellows who came back in retaliation and burned our neighbors out. He was trying to avoid trouble and to get rid of the man. I was disgusted with my dad for not beating the man up. Anyway, Dad went back into the field. I presumed he was trying to make up his mind about what he should do.

About a month before, I had bought a little .32-caliber pistol. I carried it when I ran my trap lines to dispose of animals that were in the trap—and, of course, for protection. I knew I couldn't handle this big burly man, but I loaded my pistol and put it in my pocket. I went down and got my team of horses and wagon to go and get another load of bundles. I drove by where this man was sitting with the wagon and team. I tied the reins of my horses, got down off the wagon, and walked over to the man. I asked, "Why don't you get out and pitch bundles like you should?" He answered, "Kid, this ain't your business, and I won't pitch bundles 'til your dad pays me $1.50." I said, "If you don't like the job, quit." He answered, "I like the job. It's the pay I don't like." I said, "I want you to get off this place. It's our place, and you leave—right now." He growled, "You damn brat, I'm gonna run this pitchfork through you. We'll see how damn fast you can run!" He grabbed his pitchfork with the tines pointed at my belly.

I pulled out my pistol and said, "Another step, you bastard, and I'll let daylight through that big belly of yours." That guy actually turned pale. Had I been a man, he would have realized I might not shoot. But a kid was sometimes unpredictable. He stabbed the pitchfork into the ground. I said, "Are you leavin' now, or do I start shootin'?" He glared at me and walked away. I stood there a little while, then took my team of horses and wagon, and followed him until he walked out of the field, over the hill, and back toward town.

I put my load of bundles in my wagon and drove over to the thresher. My dad came over to me and said, "Lloyd, I saw you talking to that man who had my horses and wagon. I noticed him leaving and going over the hill while you followed him with your horses and wagon. What happened?" I told him. He said, "God a'mighty, Lloyd, did you really pull a gun on that fellow?" I said, "Yeah, Pop, and if he hadn't left or if he had come any closer with that pitchfork, I was gonna let some daylight through him." Pop said, "Well, I'll be damned! I'm glad he's gone, but how do we know he won't be back tonight?" I said, "Let's put two or three guards out with guns. If he comes back, we can protect our property." We did that. We had no more trouble.

Within a week some of the same troublemakers were in Aberdeen. We saw where there was a pitched battle between the troublemakers and the settlers. The actual results of the battle I do not know, but I remember a few days later that the head of Industrial Workers of the World issued a statement to the newspaper that he was ordering all the IWW out of the state of South Dakota. He declared that they were going to let the farmers' crops be lost.

We finished the harvest and had no more problems. Those troublemakers had learned that the settlers would fight to defend their property.

THE EMPTY GUN (1908)

Much has been said about the empty gun. I had it brought home to me vividly.

In Dakota we had a lot of foxes and some wolves. The wolves were usually timber wolves. If one of them got in a flock of sheep, it did tremendous damage. Everyone did everything they could to eliminate these animals, especially the wolves.

Everybody had a pony and virtually lived on horseback. We could really ride. The ponies were so well trained that they usually had only a little rope around their necks. No one used a saddle except to work cattle. If we went for a ride, it was always bareback.

Those little mustangs were so well trained that if you leaned to the left, your pony turned left. If you leaned to the right, your pony turned right. It was country with a lot of game, and we were all taught to hunt on ponies. Like the Indians, we would shoot from horseback rather than on foot, especially when we were running wolves.

A half-dozen of us had gotten together one Sunday afternoon. About half of us were carrying rifles. I had mine, a .22 special. We had hound and Airedale dogs with us. We spotted a wolf that had left a thicket of small timber headed for a larger cover. We let out a whoop and our ponies lit out on a dead run, everyone firing at random. Our dogs were running the wolf, but he was far enough in the lead to make the dogs safe from the bullets. Every once in a while a lucky bullet would hit the wolf—until we finally killed him. We came home from this wolf hunt and, as was customary in that country, we were laughing and talking and cleaning and oiling our rifles after a successful hunt.

These were repeating rifles, and I had taken mine apart, which, in turn, lets all the cartridges spill out of the magazine. So I knew the gun was empty. I loved that rifle and was very proud of it. As I started putting it back together, I got to wondering if there was any detectable compression of air in the barrel of the rifle when you pulled the trigger and the hammer drove the firing pin into the barrel. I knew there had to be some compression but wondered if it was detectable. So, knowing the gun was empty, I stood it on its stock, put my hand over the end of the barrel, cocked the rifle, and was ready to pull the trigger when it dawned on me that there were so many calluses on my hand that even if there was the anticipated compression, with the calluses so heavy, I couldn't feel it. So, since I still wanted to find out, I leaned over and put my cheek over the end of the barrel and made it airtight. I reached down with my right hand to pull the trigger. But the barrel of the gun was too long! I couldn't hold my cheek flat over the end of the barrel and still reach the trigger. Disappointed, I put my hand back over the end of the barrel and pulled the trigger.

The bullet tore through my left hand! I realized I had shot myself through the hand! I picked up the rifle and threw it as far as I could. I raced home and came through the door on a dead run. Mom and Pop saw the blood streaming from my hand. Fathers and mothers were the doctors for their children in those days, but this time was different. My dad hollered to the other boys, "Get that team of horses on the surrey!" We went to White on a dead run. At the doctor's office we found the doctor taking his customary Sunday afternoon nap. We woke him up. He took a look at my hand and said, "Son, I think that bullet went clean through and out your hand." He went out to the chicken house and cut off a piece of wire about ten inches long. He came back to the house and made a swab out of a piece of cloth. Then he wound the swab around the end of the wire like you would make a cleaning rod. He dipped it in a bottle of iodine and told me to hold out my hand—which I did—and he ran the swab all the way through my hand. DAMN!

The bones were broken in the center of my hand where the bullet went through. Of course when he attempted to draw the swab back, the broken bones resented that. He gave two or three jerks. I said, "Pull it all the way through, then do it again." He said, "I suppose that would work better." So he did that two or three times. Then he put a little cotton on top of my hand and put the rest of the cloth like a bandage on top of the cotton. He wrapped it up and told me to come back to see him in about a week.

In about a week, my mother and dad took the bandage off, took the cotton off, and bathed my hand. They decided it was getting well and that I didn't need to see the doctor again.

After that I learned to treat every rifle like it was loaded. I have told a lot of little kids about my experience with an empty gun. They were always impressed when I showed them where the bullet went in and where it came out.

ICE SKATING (1910)

In the early days in South Dakota, it seemed to me that we learned to ice skate as soon as we learned to walk. Even in below zero weather and, especially when the moon was full, we would get up skating parties. We would skate on the lakes and rivers into the wee hours of the morning.

When the snow was well packed in the winter and the lake frozen, one of our favorite sports was to take an old car up on a hill overlooking the lake. We would get some of the girls in the car and drive down the hill as fast as the car would go. On top of the snow and the lake's clear ice, it was smooth enough to drive at speeds of forty, fifty, even sixty miles an hour.

As soon as you hit the clear ice, you could slam your foot on the brake. One wheel would always hold better than the other, and in those days, the brake was mainly on the rear wheels. Immediately, when you touched the brake, the car would spin wildly. The fun was that the car, while spinning, was still sailing forward at tremendous speed across the lake. Sometimes the lake was two to three miles across. You never heard such screaming in your life as the girls would do. They would grab everything in range to hang onto. This was one way of forcing them to hug you, whether they wanted to or not.

STRATEGY (1911)

When I was growing up in the Dakotas, most fellows had a pair of boxing gloves. Ordinarily, two boys would put on their boxing gloves and not stop until one or the other wasn't able to get up after being knocked down. All of this was done in good will, but with the determination to win.

There was a young fellow who was a couple of years older and slightly larger than I was. I thought I could possibly handle him, but wasn't sure. I think he had the same feeling about me. Neither one of us pressed the issue.

Some of the boys asked him if he thought he could handle me. I heard his reply was, "I think so, but I don't know." So I said the same thing. This is the way it went for about two years. A showdown was inevitable.

During this time, three friends and I decided to follow the harvest together. To save our money, which we had very little of, we rode empty boxcars on the railroads heading to the country, where we had heard we could get jobs picking and shelling corn. We did find work following a four-hole corn-sheller. This is the way it worked. Corn had been picked and was in stacks as high as the corn could be thrown with shovels—hundreds of yards in length—thousands of bushels of corn. Two men would be on one side of this big stack of corn, shoveling the corn to the sheller, and two men on the other side—all working as fast as they could. The big sheller could shell the corn almost as fast as four men could shovel the corn to it.

For recreation, I had my boxing gloves with me. I spent a lot of time boxing whenever I could find someone who would put on another pair. I was getting a lot of experience, gaining a little weight, and building quite a reputation on the road.

My challenger was building quite a reputation at home. Wherever I was, I made it home for my birthday. Mom always had a whipped cream cake especially for me on November 24. Later my wife, Dolly, and my daughter, Betty, kept up the tradition.

This meant I would be home on Thanksgiving when the usual gang got together. This particular year they decided the main attraction of my homecoming should be a boxing match between this young fellow and me. They told me it was all arranged, so I couldn't refuse!

Late in the afternoon of Thanksgiving Day, when the gang was all together, they told us they had a ring all squared off with rope and that we just had to have this boxing match. He didn't refuse. I didn't, either. The next thing we knew, they were tying the gloves on us. This was to be a match by stopwatch and by rounds.

In those days, it was popular for young men to wear their hair in what was called a pompadour. It meant you let your hair grow long and combed it straight back. I was always a little embarrassed because my hair was coarse and thick and stood straight up. All I could do was keep it cropped like a hairbrush rather than in a pompadour. You guessed it! He had a pompadour.

We had been boxing five or six rounds. I thought it was about even, but maybe I had more endurance than he had. He was probably thinking "just a matter of time 'til I teach this kid a lesson." I noticed, while boxing, that when I would crowd him and do considerable punching, that heavy pompadour of his would work forward on his head and start coming down over his eyes. The sun was getting low in the afternoon. I saw that each time his hair would start down over his face, he would throw his head back.

It was time to use some strategy. I would work him around so that he was facing the sun and then crowd him. If his hair started falling over his eyes, he would throw his head back, and the sun would be in his eyes. It worked great! He dropped his head to throw it back. I put everything I had into a right cross to his jaw and hit him a terrific blow right on the side of his nose.

I was shocked to see the blood stream from his mouth and nose! His nose was broken right between his eyes and had moved about an inch to the right! Immediately, he wanted to jump up and kill me. The boys stopped the fight. He was laid on his back. His nose was fairly well straightened with a small stick placed on each side to hold it in place. It was taped so that his nose could not move, and it healed that way.

I always had mixed emotions about it, because I had taken a little bit of an advantage over him. I rationalized it by figuring that I had the right, like a general in combat, to plan the battle and use strategy.

BENT BARREL (1912)

My father came to America from Denmark when he was nineteen years old. He left behind his entire family.

One day, many years later, he received a letter from his brother in Denmark telling my dad that he had a young son, Magnus, who had gotten completely out of control. Since my uncle's health was very bad, he asked my dad if he could send this son to the United States. It would give the boy a new start and could change his life. My dad and mother talked it over for several days and finally wrote a letter saying that Magnus could come and live in our home.

Now, my dad and mother, with five boys and two girls, had the job of keeping them all busy. It helped to keep them out of mischief. Many times my dad regretted ever having permitted Magnus to come because he was hardheaded and did pretty much as he pleased. He was completely irresponsible.

One time he borrowed a shotgun from Dad—one that my father thought a lot of and took excellent care of. He told Carl (the name we gave Magnus) he would let him borrow the gun but to take care of it.

Carl and I hitched a horse to a cart and went hunting together. I was driving the horse. Carl had taken the gun out of the gun case to be ready if prairie chickens or any other game flew up along the side of the road. Carl, careless with the gun, let it slip down to where the end of the barrel hit the road. With the forward movement of the buggy, it bent the barrel of the gun in a half circle.

We both hated to tell my dad what had happened. It was really Carl's fault and not mine, so I was wondering how he was going to tell him.

Well, when we got home, Carl didn't tell Dad at all. He simply set it in the gun cabinet—no cleaning—nothing. Naturally, my dad went in to see his gun after he had loaned it out. He was shocked when he noticed the bent barrel. Dad asked Carl, "What did you do to my shotgun?" Carl answered, "Uncle Peter, everyone has a gun that shoots straight. Now you have one that shoots around a corner. I'm not gonna charge you nothin' for the improvement."

This was just one of many such incidents while my dad's nephew lived with us.

RIPE APPLES (1912)

One time my cousin Carl, my brother Elmer, and I hitched a horse to a buggy and headed for Oak Lake to do some hunting. We intended to stay overnight and make a two-day hunting trip out of it. We carried a couple loaves of bread and other provisions to cook over the campfire. While driving by a pretty, late apple orchard by the side of the road, we all decided it would be nice to have a few of those apples to munch on.

We knew the old fellow who owned the apple orchard was pretty crabby. He protected his apples from people who liked to sample them—with a shotgun. So we carefully scanned the orchard and the house. We decided the old man was probably in the house. Since it was dark, he wouldn't be out any more that evening.

We drove past the orchard a little way, tied our horse where he would not be seen, and went back. Our idea was to pick a few of the apples, drop them in the front of our shirts, and head back to the horse and buggy. We ran to about the center of the orchard, where the apples were the reddest, and began picking them.

Carl looked up and said, "Those high up are better than these we can reach. I'll climb up and knock 'em down." He had just gotten up in the tree when Elmer whispered, "Here he comes!" I looked up and could see his boots not more than fifty feet away. Elmer and I lit out as hard as we could run, not making any noise. We heard the old man talking to himself, muttering, "I know they're here. I heard 'em."

Elmer and I got to the edge of the orchard where the old man had a fence. We slipped under it and ran for the horse and cart. We knew he would come to the road and see the horse and cart, so the only thing we could do was untie the horse, jump in the cart, and take off. We drove probably a mile before we realized Carl didn't know where to meet us. Oh, well, he knew we were going to Oak Lake, still about five miles away. So we drove on. A couple of hours later a very ill-tempered cousin walked up. He acted like he had been abandoned!

He and Elmer wound up in a good fistfight. I was only a spectator.

I'D NEVER LET YOU DROWN (1912)

Only a short while after the apple gathering incident, Carl would turn the tables a little. He and I decided to go duck hunting. We drove a horse and buggy to Lake Ponsett, cooked a meal with some game we had shot on the way, and lay down to sleep on the sand by the lake.

The next morning there was a strong breeze blowing. There were trees along the south shore that broke the wind, though, so we paid little attention to anything but ducks. While walking along, we saw a flock of ducks heading in toward a point just in front of us. We immediately took cover and waited. As they came into range, we both fired several times. Seven ducks were lying in the water, but they were drifting away from shore. I was raised never to shoot game unless you got it in, regardless of where it fell. The only thing to do was strip my clothes off and swim out and get those ducks.

I jumped into the water and swam out. The waves were high, and the ducks would come into and out of sight, depending on whether they were in waves or on top. I got to the first duck and took the wing feathers in my teeth, and added the second one. By the time I had gotten the third duck anchored by his wing feathers, I looked toward shore and realized I was nearly half a mile out. The wind was blowing a gale, and I was rapidly drifting out on a lake that was several miles across!

I quickly decided that I didn't need those ducks—that I'd do well to get myself back to shore against this gale. I was a good swimmer, but instead of taking long and easy strokes as I knew I should, I kicked into high gear and swam as hard as I could. I watched the waves, sure I was losing ground, so I fought it that much harder. In a matter of probably half an hour, I had completely played myself out. I had made no headway.

Wait! Down the shore of the lake a few hundred yards were a couple of boats with oars in them. I screamed to Carl to get a boat and row out to me. But with the wind blowing the high waves, he was just sitting there watching me swim. He never made a move. I realized he couldn't see or hear what my predicament was. I had completely played myself out and began to sink. My arms and legs were almost helpless from the battle I had had. I started down, knowing I was going to drown, but before my head went under water, my knees struck a large rock. I scrambled up on the rock and carefully felt with my feet. As near as I could tell, it had to be a rock eight or ten feet in diameter, covered with about two and a half to three feet of water.

I realized what a serious mistake I had made. Now, if I swam with common sense, I could make the shore. If I didn't play myself out, if necessary, I could turn and go to the other side of the lake. So I rested.

Finally, I slid off this precious rock, took long easy strokes, and realized I was making headway. About half an hour later, I waded out on the bank.

I was furious at Carl for not coming to help me and told him so. I said, "If I hadn't hit that rock, you'd have sat here on the damn bank and watched me drown." He answered, "No, Lloyd, I'd never let you drown." "Sure," I yelled, "How were you gonna stop it?"

Carl answered, "I'd shoot you before I let you drown."

THE PRETTY LITTLE BRUNETTE (1908–1984)

I had often heard that things that have happened are not ever really forgotten, but remain forever in the mind, and it merely takes certain and sometimes unusual circumstances to unlock the memory.

In the spring of the year in Dakota, we would move our cattle to graze in the hill country. This was done by driving the cattle across country by horseback. Then in the fall of the year, before the bad weather set in, these cattle would be brought back across country where they would winter better. In those days, all cattle were moved by horseback. Moving them took us by a country schoolhouse. One day the school teacher, seeing the large herd of cattle, knew she could not keep the attention of the pupils so she decided it would be better to dismiss them and let them watch the cattle drive. We were boys on horseback driving the cattle. When we saw boys and girls our ages, we let the cattle graze and we did a lot of visiting and getting acquainted. I noticed a cute little brunette that I became very much interested in.

Some years later, when I had gone into the service and had come back home on furlough, they had a barn dance, which I attended. I was still recuperating from a serious motorcycle accident so I was really not doing a great deal of dancing. Both my legs and ankles had been broken in the accident. The music was being furnished that night by this little brunette's older sister, who was recently married, and her young husband. The sister played the piano and her young husband played the violin. All of a sudden this little brunette ran across the dance floor to where I was and said, "Lloyd, this is going to be our dance. I talked to my sister and brother-in-law and told them to play my song. I was going to dance it with you because this is ladies' choice." I told her I was not doing a good job of dancing because I was still recuperating from injuries from the motorcycle wreck. She laughed and said, "We'll get by, and I have hard toes on my shoes." We began to dance and she began to sing. The song was evidently not very popular because I had never heard it before or since. The song was sentimental and very lovely. I told her it was beautiful and that she had done a fabulous job singing it. I also said I really thought she was probably the prettiest little flirt I had ever known. Her answer to me was that she was not a flirt and if I would come and see her when I came back from the service, she would prove to me that she meant what she said. We both laughed, and I told her I didn't know what better thoughts a fellow could have on a night when he was leaving for the service than to realize that such a lovely little girl would be waiting for him when he came back. So our conversation ended.

Sixty-six years passed and I was making plans to attend the centennial in White, South Dakota, where my father and mother had homesteaded and helped lay out the town in 1884. I had left South Dakota to go into the service and had not been back to the town of White since 1918. For years I had subscribed to the White *Leader*, which was the weekly paper published in town at the time I left in 1918. It is still the town paper. I had written to several acquaintances I had made through the years and asked them to give me the names of people that were still there who belonged to the old families that I remembered as a boy. So I learned that most of them were no longer with us, but I was pleased to learn that probably half a dozen of those I knew sixty-six years ago were still there. They would have to be between eighty-five and ninety-five years old. As I was making plans for the centennial, I learned that not only was the girl who had played the piano still there, but also the pretty little brunette. So I made up my mind that I would write several letters to others that I had learned still lived in the vicinity of the town and invite them all to join us for dinner while we were there. I also decided that when everyone had gathered I was going to thank them for coming and then tell them about the last time I was in White. I would describe the barn dance and mention that I now knew this pretty little brunette happened to be present at the dinner, assuming that she would be there. Did she remember the incident as I did and the song which I had never heard before or since? Would she favor us by singing the song for those who had attended the dinner? So I began building my plans for some kind of a reunion along these lines.

A few days before the centennial I received my White *Leader*, and as I opened it I noticed an obituary. It was the little brunette. Needless to say I was greatly shocked, and the thing that is extremely interesting is that the words and the tune of that song came back clearly to my mind. I asked my daughter, Betty, to come to the office. I told her the story and sang her the song.

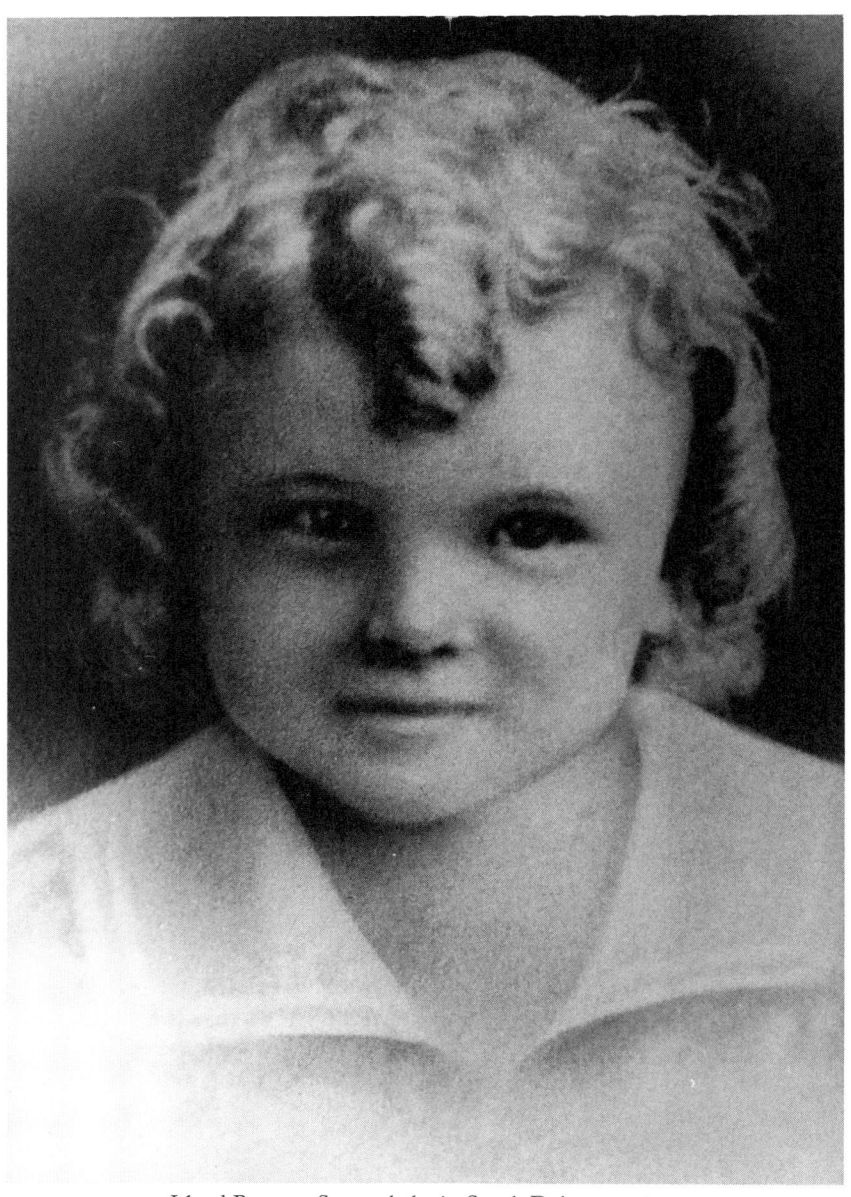

Lloyd Bentsen Sr. as a baby in South Dakota, c. 1894.

Lloyd Bentsen, back row, fourth from left, and his classmates at school in White, South Dakota, c. 1907.

A Christmas card Lloyd Bentsen sent to his grandmother, c. 1906.

Lloyd Bentsen, standing, third from left; his brother Dietz, standing, far right; his brother Alton, seated, far left; and his brother Elmer, seated, second from left, c. 1915.

The Bentsen family, c. 1915. Back row, from left, Dietz, Lloyd, Edna, Laurel, Elmer, and Alton. Front row, Peter and Tena Bentsen.

Lloyd Bentsen, on crutches after his motorcycle accident in 1915, with his parents and sister Laurel, left.

Tena Bentsen, c. 1952.

Peter Bentsen, c. 1945.

Lloyd Bentsen, second row, fourth from left, with his unit during World War I.

Lloyd Bentsen in his Army uniform during World War I.

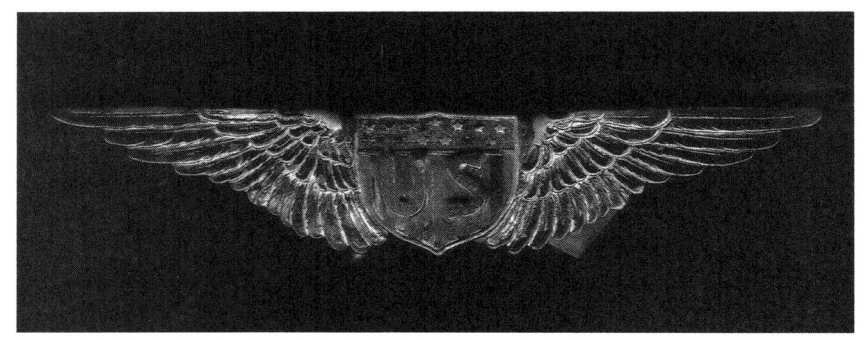

Lloyd Bentsen's wings from World War I.

Edna Ruth Colbath at the piano, c. 1917.

Pilot

103 ON A HARLEY-DAVIDSON TWIN MOTORCYCLE (1915)

I was having a lot of pleasure riding and racing a Harley-Davidson Twin motorcycle. There were very few of them in existence at that time.

I met a young man who was also riding and racing. His motorcycle was what was known as an Excelsior Twin. We immediately became rivals—so much so that we agreed to race at the county fair, which was to take place during the next couple of weeks.

So, the first day I had off I decided to tune up my motorcycle and get ready for the race. The track we were to race on was a dirt track. Of course, in those days all the roads we traveled were dirt roads. I took my motorcycle and went to a place where I knew there was a long, smooth piece of road, where I could check it out completely.

There was a small air jet on the carburetor that could be opened at high speed. It would add another two or three miles per hour to the speed of the motorcycle, but I had to know when was the right time to open this jet and just how much to open it. I didn't intend to lose that race.

I got to the top of a long slope. I had my motorcycle where the speedometer was recording slightly in excess of 101 miles per hour. Then, lying down between the handlebars and watching the speedometer, I began to test the variance of speed as I opened the jet on the carburetor. I picked up another couple of miles per hour speed.

When I looked down the road, I saw a horse and buggy pulling in from a side road. This irritated me because I needed at least a full mile. It would take fifteen or twenty minutes before that horse and buggy would come to the next crossroad and get out of my way. Just about the time I had reached this conclusion, they saw the motorcycle coming and turned the horse to a side road that paralleled the main road. I appreciated that very much.

Again, lying low over the handlebars, I began checking my carburetor and speedometer, glancing up every few seconds to see if the road remained clear. The last time I looked up, the horse, frightened of the contraption coming down the road, was rearing up on his hind legs in an effort to leap across the road. I was traveling at approximately 103 miles per hour, and was about fifty feet from the horse and buggy. I swerved the motorcycle enough to miss the horse and slammed on all the brake I had—then I plowed into the front of the buggy. My body and the motorcycle went through the buggy like a bullet.

The motorcycle was a total wreck. The body of the buggy had come loose from the springs and was sitting upright on the road. From the impact to where my body lay in the road was 127 feet, some thirty feet farther than the motorcycle had gone.

I sat up in the middle of the road. All my clothes had been stripped from my body so that I had only a leather belt around my waist and leather shoes on my feet. The rest of me was almost completely skinned and cut so that I was bleeding everywhere. The damp blood all over my body had picked up dirt and dust as I rolled up the road. It looked like I had bathed in mud.

I was completely numb. I tried to assess the damage. My right leg was twisted up like a rope, and bones were sticking through the flesh in many places. My ankle was broken, and the foot looked like it was on backward. I don't know why, but I reached over with my right hand to straighten the foot out. My hand was broken so that my fingers simply folded back. I reached down with my left hand to straighten my foot out. When I attempted to lift it, my shoulder slipped up two or three inches, and I realized it was broken. Completely disgusted and completely numb, I took my left leg and kicked the other foot out straight. Then I looked down and saw where something sharp had torn the front of my body open. It was full of mud from the dust, dirt, and blood. The thing that most concerned me was the blood spurting through the holes in my right leg. I realized the artery had to be cut in several places.

About that time I realized that a little girl and her mother had been in the buggy. The little girl was standing by my side and asking if there was anything she could do to help. I told her she might be able to save my life. "My artery's cut! A few minutes and I'll be out of blood!" She said, "Tell me what to do." I said, "If you can, take my leather belt. Wrap it 'round my right leg good and tight. Get one of those broken buggy spokes lying back there. Put it through the belt and twist it up real tight." It must have been quite an ordeal for her, because the belt was covered with blood and mud. As she put it around my leg, her hands were completely covered. She put in the buggy spoke and tried to twist it, but it didn't stop the surging of the blood. I told her to run back to the buggy and pick up some of my clothes that had been torn off, to twist them in a hard knot, to put them under the belt on the inside of my thigh, to press them where the artery was, then to twist the belt tight with the buggy spoke. She did. The surging stopped, but it seemed to me that I was bleeding everywhere.

Strange as it may sound—remember this was a time when you wouldn't see an automobile once a week—an automobile came down the road. Two young men jumped out and asked if they could do anything to help. I said, "Get me to a hospital." They carefully picked me up, laid me on the floor of their seven-passenger car and headed for Brookings, eighteen miles away. Feeling was beginning to come back to normal. Pain became a reality. When we got to the hospital, they slipped me out of the car onto a stretcher. This was probably about eleven o'clock in the morning, but I remember as they carried me through the door of the hospital that everything was turning dark. I remember saying to one of the men carrying the stretcher, "It's getting night." Then, of course, I passed out. My recollection is that about fifteen or twenty hours later, I had been cleaned up as well as they could manage. They had set my hand and shoulder. They sewed up the cuts, but the doctors had not decided what to do about my right leg.

When I had left home that morning and bid my mother goodbye, I had noticed her beautiful luxurious head of dark hair. She was tall and slender and could stand up perfectly straight. Her hair was so long that when she sat combing her hair and it hung down her back, four inches would be lying on the floor behind her. When I woke up in the hospital after the accident, I was shocked to see all the white hair sprinkled through the beautiful dark hair.

My mother and dad were there along with several members of the family. The doctors told my dad that there was a possibility they could operate on my leg. If they could wire the bones close enough, they might grow back together. He asked me what I thought. I told him I wanted them to go ahead as quickly as possible. They scheduled the operation for the next morning.

After the operation the doctors would give me no encouragement. They said they had done everything they could, but the bones were so badly shattered they thought it would take a miracle for me to walk on the leg again.

I stayed in that hospital several months while my wounds were healing and bones were knitting. They had a large rack, or form, that lay on the bed over which my right leg rested with heavy weights tied to the foot. They had to keep the muscles from contracting and making the bones slip past each other. After about three months, the doctors said the bones were beginning to knit. It looked encouraging because there had been no infection—a rare thing before the protection of antibiotics.

Strangely enough, though this was a small town, there was a hospital. Next to the hospital was what they called the Nurses Home. Most of the time I was in this hospital, there were from ten to twenty-four student nurses with only two or three other patients. These student nurses were approximately the same age I was, and they all had to practice being nurses. Certainly, nobody ever got more attention than I did. Usually, they would come up to my room and make taffy, fudge, or popcorn balls, and we would have a party all night long. Then, in the morning, because I hadn't slept, I would sleep most of the day. I certainly thought a hospital was about as close to heaven as you could get, and these nurses, some lovely angels. That hospital was a great place to be!

WILLIAM AND CHARLIE MAYO AND A GOOD LEG (1916)

A few months had passed since my motorcycle wreck. I was still in the hospital and the doctors were encouraged because, other than my right leg, I was fine. There had been no infection, and the bones were knitting in the leg. But I wondered.

One morning when the doctors came in, I asked them to measure my left leg from the hipbone to the ankle and then measure my right leg in the same manner. They told me the right leg was two and a half inches shorter than the left. I said, "The weights you're using aren't heavy enough. I want the leg re-broken and stretched out to the right length. We'll start over." They told me that they would talk to my dad and mother about it. They didn't think that it was the right thing to do and that I should be satisfied to have a good leg. The difference could be made up by the type shoe I could wear. I would have none of that!

When my dad got there the next morning, I didn't tell him the doctors had measured my legs. I asked him to measure them, and he did. I saw, as he measured the broken leg, his face pale. I asked, "How much, Pop, is it short?" He answered, "Lloyd, I don't think it's serious." I said, "It is! There's two inches difference, and I'm not going to have it. I've already talked to the doctors. I want it re-broken and stretched out to its full length. I am not going to be crippled."

We had a lot of arguments.

Finally, the doctors went along reluctantly with what I wanted to do. They agreed to re-break the leg. I presumed they would put it across a heavy timber, and with one swing-snap, it would be broken.

Now, as a youngster I had taken a great deal of pride in reading the history of the Vikings and Norsemen. I felt because my dad and mother were both natives of Denmark, I was a full-blooded Viking. Those Vikings had nerve, and they were insensitive to pain. Well, I belonged to the same crowd. So, I insisted the doctors break the leg and not use morphine, that I could take it. Finally, after a lot of arguments, and me being the stubborn Viking I thought I was, we began.

I soon realized we weren't talking about putting my leg over a board and snapping it. Instead, they first removed the weights from the foot, then straightened the leg out and removed the frame it had been hanging over. Two doctors grasped the leg above the thigh and held it rigid while the third doctor began rocking the foot from side to side. This way the new growth between the bones would give way without the chance of breaking any more bones. It seemed to me it took hours. The pain was intense! They were finally through. The bed was soaked with my perspiration. I had gritted my teeth so tight that I couldn't open my mouth. It took days before the muscles in my jaws relaxed so that I could eat. But they had re-broken the leg.

Two more months proved that the leg was not going to grow back together. It had been so badly shattered that every few days one, two, or three little red spots would show up on the leg. They would open it up and pull out another piece of shattered bone. The doctors finally told us there was no use wasting any more time. The leg would have to be removed. But, if we wanted to try anything further, we should go to Rochester, Minnesota, where, at that time there was what was called the Mayo Brothers (Clinic), run by William and Charlie Mayo.

My mother went with me, and we traveled to Rochester. We were soon talking to the bone specialists. One of them told us that progress had been made in bone surgery and that he believed the best thing in my case was to remove all the shattered bone and to replace both the shinbone and the tibia (as I remember it) with new bone. He said our only real enemy was infection (this was long before we had penicillin). He said, "I don't worry much about infection in your case, because with all you've been through and, having had no infection heretofore, I believe we have a very good chance of avoiding infection in this operation." He went on to say, "To be very frank about it, practically the whole gamble is infection. If you do have infection, you will lose the knee joint, because we would have to remove the leg above the knee. If you don't have infection, we have a strong chance of making a good leg, but probably never as strong as the other. You might always walk with a cane, but that's a lot better than a peg." In those days, there were no artificial limbs. What they used was a peg on the stump of the leg. It was strapped onto the thigh and had a rubber tip so it wouldn't slip. This was what he meant by the peg. I told him I was willing to gamble the joint. They scheduled the operation.

I actually looked forward to all the attention I would again be receiving from all the nurses after the operation. I was due for a rude awakening. In the little hospital where I had been—with a couple dozen student nurses—and me the only patient much of the time, well, they needed the practice, and I was pretty well taken care of! But in this hospital, with hundreds of patients and the overworked nurses, I soon lost my illusion of attention.

They were very efficient, and I got the attention I needed, but there was no taffy-pulling or making of fudge or popcorn balls.

Finally, after many months, I was ready to leave the hospital on a pair of crutches. I went to the business office and asked for my bill. My doctor came out and asked if I had any money. I told him, "I don't have but a few hundred dollars, but I hope to be working again soon. I wanted to know how much I owed so I could pay it off or, at least, get started on paying it off." He replied, "We don't know if we've finished this job yet. Why don't you go on home and let me know how you get along? Then we'll talk about our bill."

A couple of years passed. I was in the Air Service (called the Signal Corps then). I flew in an airplane from Mineola, Long Island, New York, to Rochester, Minnesota, to see my doctor. I came in there in my uniform. I said, "Dr. Henderson, do you know who I am?" He said, "Don't tell me who you are, you're Bentsen from Dakota. This is fabulous."

I spent two and a half hours at the hospital with the doctors, seeing what they had done with bone surgery. It was so new at that time and had been organized by Will and Charlie Mayo. I met them when I was there. I said, "I don't have any money but I'm a second lieutenant and I will be getting a raise pretty soon. I have a $10,000 risk insurance policy and I'll make that out to you, but I think I'll be back because I can shoot pretty good. I want you to send me a bill so I'll know how much I owe you." They said, "Fine, leave us your address and we'll send you a bill."

I got back to New York and got a very official looking letter from the Mayo Clinic that worried the hell out of me. I opened the end of that letter and started slipping that letter out. I saw a dollar sign then a two and a five, I thought I had gotten by with a bill for $2,500.00, then I saw a zero, a period and oo. I had gotten a bill for $250.00.

Many years later I received a letter advertising for the Mayo Clinic in Rochester, Minnesota. I wrote them a letter saying you want to tell me something about the Mayo Clinic? Let me tell you something about the Mayo Clinic. They called and asked if they could publish my story in their newspaper. I said I had no objection.

YOU CAN'T MEASURE UP (1917)

I traveled home from Mayo Brothers on a train. My leg, mangled in a motorcycle wreck with a horse and buggy, was at last healing. I could walk—with crutches. I bought a jalopy, an old Ford car that cost me $150.

I had always been an adventurous, thrill-hungry youngster. The war was going on. An older brother was already in the service, as well as my cousin, Magnus. It concerned me that here was a great opportunity for me to serve the country that I dearly loved, in the greatest adventure imaginable, and I was laid up waiting for these bones to heal! I think my principal worry was that the war might end before I could do my part. And I was missing out on the thrills and adventure that I had been reading about in wars of past generations.

As soon as I could throw away my crutches and put some weight on my leg, I got around fairly well on a cane. I began haunting the recruiting stations. One day I picked up a weekly paper where there was a notice that an examination would be held in Minneapolis. The lucky ones would be called "America's Young Supermen." It was tied to aviation. Those who were successful would be America's flyers in the war—maybe even the aces. It gave the time and place this examination would take place.

I got in my jalopy and drove to Minneapolis, Minnesota, probably two hundred miles from home, and went to the office building where the examination was to take place. In probably an hour's time, fifteen or twenty young men about my age had gathered for the same purpose.

I think the building was a part of some college or university. In a short while a middle-aged man came in and invited us into another room, where we were to give a short résumé of our education, experience, and qualifications. I had looked over the group of young fellows who had gathered and, having in the back of my mind the advertisement that was calling for supermen, I figured I had the best chance of anyone there. My idea of a superman was the man who was in the best physical condition, the man who could probably win in a wrestling or a boxing match and—because it was associated with the war—the man who was a marksman with a pistol, rifle, and shotgun. I certainly seemed to have the best qualifications. Not having gone to school very much, I didn't give my education much thought. I figured a guy could outdo the enemy in combat even if his formal education was brief. After I wrote my résumé, I felt pretty secure in what I had told them. I was equally certain that if anybody in this crowd was selected, I would certainly be the first. Deep down inside, I felt a little sorry for any of the boys who would not make it.

We left that room and went into another. The same middle-aged man came in and told us to strip to the waist for a physical examination. We did, and again I felt pretty secure. In a few minutes, another man walked in the room, looked over the crowd, then turned and walked directly to me. I wasn't surprised because I thought I would be the first one they would select with all the qualifications I had. Again, I felt sorry for the other boys.

This man asked, "Is your name Bentsen?" I answered, "Yes, sir!" He said, "You can put on your clothes. You can't measure up to the standard we require for the Aviation Section of the Signal Corps." (This was the organization our flyers belonged to long before the Air Force came into being.)

I couldn't believe what I had heard. I realized tears were coming into my eyes, which I couldn't stop. I tried to ask, "What did you say?" but I noticed my throat was closing up. I was actually crying, which embarrassed me very much. I turned around, grabbed my cane, and left the room with tears running down my cheeks.

I got in my jalopy, and I think if there had been an enemy recruiting station across the street, I would have gone in and enlisted. Here I was, wanting to serve my country, risk life and limb if necessary, and they were telling me I couldn't measure up!

"AS LONG AS AMERICA MAKES THEM LIKE YOU..." (1917)

My heart was set on air battle as the greatest thrill that any war ever had, or could, produce. Those words, "You can't measure up!" burned.

I continued haunting recruiting stations, determined to be in some branch of the service before the war ended. I must have gone to at least a hundred recruiting stations, only to be turned down each time and told to come back when I could get along without the cane.

One day, driving through the city of Sioux Falls, South Dakota, I saw a beige sign on a building. It showed Uncle Sam pointing down at the street, and it said, "Uncle Sam Wants You." I looked up, and the finger was pointing straight at me. I pulled in at the curb and read the finer print, which wound up by saying this was the U.S. Recruiting Office.

I walked inside, using my cane. The man sitting at the desk was a corporal. The two stripes on his sleeve meant nothing to me at that time, except that he was in uniform. He looked at me, and with a very thick tongue, said, "Young fella, what can I do for you?" I realized he had been drinking heavily by the tone of his voice. My reply was, "I want to join the army." He asked, "Wha' branch o' the service do ya wanna join?" I didn't know there were any branches, so I answered, "I don't give a damn—just so it fights." He squinted his eyes and with the same thick voice said, "How would ya like to join the Hurdlers of Death?" I said, "Fine, what is it?" He answered, "Motorcycle dispatchers on the front lines." I said, "Fine. Right down my alley. I'm a motorcycle racer, that's how I got busted up." He shook his head, "Don't believe I should do that. You'll get over there and jump a shell hole, throw your leg out to catch your balance, and break it all over again. Think I oughta put you in Aviation." I was astonished—and very pleased! Aviation meant to me to fly and, green country boy that I was, I asked, "Can you do that?" Again, thick-tongued, he said, "I can do any damn thing I want to." I said, "Where do I sign?" He pulled out an enlistment blank, and I signed on the dotted line. My next question was, "When do I leave?" He answered, "The train down there is leaving in thirty minutes. You can be on it." I said, "Okay."

I went to a telephone in his office and made a collect call to my dad. I had no money. When he answered the telephone, I said, "Pop, I've joined the Aviation." He said, "Lloyd, you can't, not broken up like you are." My brothers were in the service, but he thought he had a cinch keeping me home because of the accident. So he said, "Come on home, and let's talk it over." I answered, "Too late, Pop. I've already signed. The train leaves in a few minutes, and I'll be on it. Tell Mom goodbye. I'll get in touch. My jalopy is standing in front of the recruiter's office in Sioux Falls, if you will send and get it." He started to argue. I said, "Bye, Pop," hung up the receiver, and headed for the depot. The next morning at daybreak, the train backed into Jefferson Barracks at St. Louis, Missouri. Immediately, as soon as the train stopped, the door of the train car was opened. We started down the walkway—me with my cane. A soldier standing out there with three stripes on his arm looked up in surprise and hollered, "Hey, Crip, what the hell are you doin' in the bunch?" I hated that word and his attitude. I yelled back, "You S.O.B. [and I didn't abbreviate], you can't call me a crip." He flared back, "You can't call me an S.O.B. I'll take you to see the colonel." Colonel meant nothing to me. I knew nothing about rank. I was like D'Artagnan in *The Three Musketeers*—a green country boy with a yen for adventure, chock full of fight, and not smart enough to be scared.

I said, "Okay with me. Let's go see your colonel." We walked probably three hundred yards and stepped into an office where a fine looking gentleman with gray hair and two eagles on his shoulders sat behind a desk. The sergeant saluted and said, "Colonel, I have a recruit here who called me an S.O.B." The colonel turned to me, "Young man, did you call the sergeant an S.O.B.?" I said, "I damn sure did, and if he calls me a crip again, I'll break his neck to boot!" He turned to the sergeant and spoke very sternly, "Sergeant, did you call this young man a crip?" The sergeant answered, "I guess I did, Colonel."

The colonel said to me, "Young man, I don't know whether I can let you stay in the service or not, since you have to use that cane." I explained to him that the grafted bone showed perfect healing and that in a few days I could throw away the cane. I unburdened my heart and told him that I had been to hundreds of recruiting stations trying to get in the service. Now I was here, and I wanted to stay—this was my only chance.

He looked at me, then got up from his desk and put his arm around my shoulders. He said, "Young man, as long as America makes them like you, we won't have a thing to worry about. Do you think you could walk up here and see me a week from today without that stick?" I said, "I will bet you I can!" His reply was, "I will bet you can, too. And if you can, I am going to let you stay in the service."

I couldn't help comparing in my mind the reception I had had from the instructor in Minneapolis, who told me I didn't measure up, to the reception I received from the colonel. I could well understand why one kind of officer could lead his men through hell while another kind could get shot in the back, during battle, by his own troops.

MY DAD HAS A GARAGE (1917)

I left Jefferson Barracks, Missouri, after about thirty days, and was sent to San Antonio, Texas. The next thing I knew we were taken to what was called a classification depot. A young officer was sitting at the desk and asking each recruit as he passed by to present his enlistment papers. The officer asked what profession or what work each recruit was familiar with. As it came my turn, I was reminded of what my thick-tongued recruiting corporal had said as I signed my enlistment papers. He said, "When you get to the classification depot, tell 'em you're a mechanic."

So, as I stood there before the young officer and he asked my experience, I wanted to tell him I was a mechanic as the recruiting corporal had suggested. But my mother had instilled in my mind so thoroughly what a terrible crime it was to lie. I couldn't lie and tell him I was a mechanic, but I hoped he would think I was when I told him, "My dad has a garage."

It was true that the only garage my dad had was the shelter that kept the snow off the car, but when I said my dad had a garage, he evidently believed what I wanted him to believe. He looked up at me and said, "There is a lot of difference between airplane motors and automobile motors."

I don't know where the words came from, but my reply was, "I agree, but the principle of internal combustion is the same in one motor as it is in another." It sounded pretty good and seemed to satisfy him. He wrote "Mechanic" on my enlistment papers.

A SNAPPY SALUTE (1917)

One day while I was taking my flying training in San Antonio, a friend said he was going home to Mission, Texas, to spend the weekend with his folks. He suggested I get a leave and join him. (This young soldier happened to become the father of Tommy Landry, coach of the Dallas Cowboys.) I asked him where Mission was, and he told me it was on the Mexican border. I got the leave, and we went hunting close to Mission where he and I each shot a buck and came back to town.

While walking down the sidewalk the next afternoon, I saw a young lady walking toward us. She had on a volunteer Red Cross uniform with silver bars on her shoulders for decoration, which, incidentally, gave her the rank of first lieutenant. She was exceedingly pretty, and, since she outranked me, at the proper distance I gave her a snappy salute, which she did not return. She dropped her head and walked right past us. I turned to Ray Landry and told him that undoubtedly she was the prettiest girl I had ever seen in my life. He said, "That's true, and she's just as pretty on the inside as she is on the outside. She lives with her grandmother and everyone who knows her loves her."

I asked, "How do I get to meet this girl?" His smart reply was I would have to go to church. "Well," I said, "it's been some time; but I can do that, too." I asked another girl I'd met to take me to church Sunday night. She said, "What church?" I said, "First Baptist Church." She answered, "Okay, we'll go to church Sunday night." We did. When the services were over, I tapped her on the shoulder and said, "Mildred—one more favor—I want to meet the little blonde singing in the choir." She said, "You snake! You didn't want a date with me, did you? You want to meet that girl." I told her I guessed that was true. Mildred said, "She's my best friend. Of course, I'll introduce you." I got one reluctant date with her before I went back to San Antonio, but we did keep in touch.

LET ELMER DO IT (1917)

After I met Edna at church I talked her into giving me a date. And my brother Elmer got a date with Marie. We borrowed a car from my dad, picked up Edna, and drove to Fort Ringgold to pick up Marie. She worked for the colonel in charge of the camp up there. The road was made for wagons so it was very narrow. You heard stories about peddlers and how they were robbed or hanged. This was pretty rough country.

I was driving the car on the way over. Edna was sitting beside me. She was studying me and wondering if she liked soldiers. We picked up Marie at Fort Ringgold and had dinner. When it was time to leave between ten and eleven o'clock Elmer walked Marie over to the boardinghouse where she was staying. I said, "Let's get in the back seat and let Elmer drive the car home." She said, "Okay," and we got in the back seat.

We started on our way home through the brush. We saw a man lying on the road. Elmer got out of the car and said, "I'm going to see what happened." I said, "This could be a holdup. Edna, you stay in the car until I come back." Then when I reached Elmer I told him I was going to have a little fun. So I went back to the car and raised the cushion seat. In those days that's where you kept the tools. I said to Edna, "Looks like an automobile has run over him. He's in pretty bad shape, lots of broken bones." Edna asked, "What are you going to do? Are you going to kill him with that hammer?" I answered, "He's in bad shape. If we move him we might kill him." She said, "Lloyd, what are you going to do?" I said, "I'm going to put him out of his misery. If we move him we will probably kill him." She put her hand over mine and said, "Let Elmer do it." That became a saying in the family, "Let Elmer do it."

We leaned the man against a mesquite tree and put a cigarette in his mouth. He never came to. I think he was drunk on marijuana. She never did forgive me for that. It was our first date.

TROUBLESHOOTER WITH A LOOSE-LEAF NOTEBOOK (1917)

I was in San Antonio a short time, then was sent to Wichita Falls. Because I was a mechanic, I was excused from all formations and assigned to a hangar. I borrowed two books out of the library, one on motors and the other on airplanes. In one of the books were the engineer's tracings of motors, showing the pistons, cylinders, carburetors, and crankshafts, as well as the firing order and position of the piston in the cylinder at the time of ignition, etc. In the other book were complete instructions on assembling the fuselage and wings of a plane (including the material it was covered with as well as the material the linen was covered and shrunk with before the plane would be put into flight).

I tried to learn everything there was about motors and airplanes. I got a loose-leaf book so I could put the loose leaf over the engineer's drawings and with a carbon paper between, trace out the drawings and have it in my book. Then, taking a pen and ink, I traced out the impression left by the carbon. My book looked almost like the original tracings. This was important a few weeks later.

I worked on the airplanes in the hangar and learned to disassemble and reassemble the motors and the carburetors. I had always been an early riser, so I would be at the hangar before reveille in the morning and still working after taps at night. I soon filled the first loose-leaf notebook, and then a second one.

There was a sergeant in charge of this hangar, and, of course, he was my boss. He was lazy and spent more time in town than he did in the hangar. As soon as he found out I was working night and day, he felt quite secure taking time off. After several weeks, I would see him only an hour a day, and sometimes only an hour every other day. Along about then, a lieutenant came into the hangar. I had learned to salute, so I saluted him. He introduced himself as Lieutenant Benson. He talked about the similarity in our names, and then he asked me where the sergeant was. I knew the sergeant was in town, but didn't want to get him in trouble, so I told the lieutenant I didn't know. He asked, "When was he last here?" I told him I had been busy and hadn't noticed. He said, "Well, I've noticed, and he's not been spending any time in this hangar or on the field since he got somebody here to do his work for him."

The next morning he came in and told me he had looked at my enlistment papers and had seen that I was a mechanic (which I was really beginning to be). He told me that hereafter I was in charge of this hangar. The sergeant was being transferred to other duties somewhere.

The superintendent of the field, or officer in charge, kept a record of the flying time recorded from each hangar. It looked like the work I had been doing was paying off because after about thirty days, this same lieutenant came into my hangar and told me that the planes assigned to this hangar had put in more flying hours than the planes assigned to the other hangars on the field. They were giving me credit for this, which pleased me very much. But I was learning that instead of getting to fly as I thought when I enlisted, I was probably going to be tied down to a mechanic's job for the duration, which I did not want.

A few days later, the same lieutenant came into the hangar and told me that with the record I had made, they were going to transfer me to troubleshooter on the field, starting next week.

Needless to say, what I knew about being a top mechanic was very limited, so when a plane came in reporting that the motor was not working properly, I would remove the jets from the carburetor and then test out the various plugs to see if it was a bad plug or a bad connection, or ice or dirt in the carburetor. That was about all I knew. So if these tests didn't produce results, I sent the plane to the shop. A smart mechanic would have tried something else, then asked them to try it out again. He wouldn't have sent it to the shop until it was actually necessary. In a short while this same lieutenant notified me that since I had been troubleshooter, they had had fewer accidents on the field. It wasn't because I was a better mechanic, but because I was sending the planes to the shop rather than having them test a faulty motor.

Shortly after this, they were having trouble in the motor division on the field. My friend the lieutenant, who evidently had an exalted opinion of my ability as a mechanic, told them what he thought of me. I was placed in charge of a section of the motor division, which was limited to rebuilding motors.

In those days, we melted babbitt, poured out our own bearings, and soldered them to the crankshaft. I knew I was moving along lots faster than I was entitled to. Neither did I want to stay on a mechanic's job.

One day my lieutenant friend told me they were opening a mechanics' training station in Minneapolis, Minnesota. It would be known as the Aviation Mechanics Training Station. They intended to train some five thousand mechanics at this school continuously. He told me that he had recommended me to go there as one of the instructors. This was completely over my head, but by moving I would be getting away from a permanent mechanic's job. I welcomed the idea.

I wrote Mom and Pop what had happened. When I got to Minneapolis, they came to see me. They were happy because they thought at least one of their sons was probably safe for the duration, but I told them, very frankly, that I didn't want the job and somehow I was going to shake loose from it. They urged me to stay, but we didn't argue.

I wanted to fly airplanes and get to the center of operations before the war ended.

THE FIVE BEST MECHANICS (1917-1918)

I was bound for Minneapolis and the new Aviation Mechanics Training Station. They had some tents put up. In these tents was an old airplane, with a laminated wooden fuselage with a four-cylinder Hall Scott motor, and a standard airplane, something I had never seen before. Someone had built it, but it probably had never flown. It was for people to study. The boys coming into this new training station—not yet open—had never seen an airplane. They were all asking questions. I was an old-time army man since I'd had several months in the army. So when I saw them asking questions, I'd go over and explain it to them. I knew it all.

I noticed a fellow standing outside the tent. He wore an officer's uniform.

In those days an officer wore a cap, and the soldiers wore campaign hats. When you saw an officer's shadow you knew the difference. I realized he was listening, so I started going into all the technical terms I'd learned about airplanes and everything else. I wanted him to think I really knew all there was to know. About that time he pulled the flap of the tent open and stepped inside. Being an old trained soldier I bellowed, "Attention," and gave him the snappiest salute I could. The other boys were stepping over their toes. They didn't know what to do because here was an old trained soldier. He came over to me and said, "As you were," and introduced himself. "I'm Captain Dawson. My daddy is a dollar-a-year man working in the Aviation Section of the Signal Corps in Washington, D.C. He was the head of [such and such] corporation before we got into the war. They sent me down here and put me in charge of this new school, and I don't know what the hell I'm doing. But we'll find out what we're doing. I heard what you were telling these boys about airplanes and motors. I need to lean on someone who knows what he is doing." I couldn't tell him I didn't know anything. So I said, "Well, I don't want to." He said, "I want to make you an instructor here and I'll have to lean on you. My daddy will see that I get the promotion and I'll see that you get the promotion." I said, "No deal." He said, "What do you mean, no deal?" I said, "I don't want to stay here." We talked for a while. He said, "Well, it's everybody's duty to do his job wherever he can do it the best and you're an A-1 mechanic. You've got to stay and we've got to have you." He went through a long rigmarole. I said, "No deal."

The captain said, "Did you bring anything along with you that we can use for a course of study 'til we get something from the government we can use? People are coming in here, and we haven't got anything to do." I said, "I have some stuff down in my barracks." So I went down and got my books. He looked at them, and he thought they were pretty good. They ought to be—they were copies from the best mechanic. I got credit for writing the book. My name was all over them. They took them and used them for the course of study for a few days while the school was trying to get open. I got credit for it. Every day we had the same feud that I didn't want to stay and he wanted me to stay.

One day he came and said, "Benny, I have one proposition." I said, "What is it?" He said, "Colonel Reinhart is putting on a Flying Circus across the United States. They have already put in an order for the five best mechanics we've got in this school. We have four thousand mechanics here, and they want us to send the best five. If you are one of those five, I'll put you in charge of the Flying Circus." I said, "Fine." "But if you are not one of those five you will stay here with no trouble." I said, "Well, we'll see about it." I took the examination the next day. Everybody knew I wrote the book—my name was all over it. That was the only thing they'd seen so nobody would judge my papers. They just marked them 100.

So I found myself traveling with Colonel Reinhart's Flying Circus.

THE WAY HE COULD FLY AND THE WAY I COULD SHOOT (1918)

It needs to be pointed out that often on our rides around the country, with the permission of the pilot, I would carry a shotgun along in the rear cockpit. Of course, these were the open cockpits of the time.

Very often in our rivers, lakes, and streams we would see a flock of ducks or other birds. We would fly close, but not too close, because they could ruin a propeller. I would stand up in the rear cockpit and blast them out of the air. This impressed the pilot very much. It caused one of these officers, when he was called for overseas duty as a fighter pilot, to request that I go with him as his gunman. When he asked if I could go, he said that the way he could fly and the way I could shoot, there wouldn't be a German plane in the sky in twenty-four hours!

I believed it, and so did he. This led, indirectly, to the flying training that I desired so very much.

THE PRINCETON GRADUATE (1918)

"The way you can shoot and the way I can fly there won't be a German plane in the sky." He asked, "Will you go?" I said, "Damn right." He said, "Okay."

Three days later he came over and said, "Benny, bad news, they denied my request." I was surprised. He said, "I ought to take somebody when we're going Over There who can shoot like you can. We would do a great job but they said, 'No deal.' So I can't take you along. Can I do anything for you before I leave?" I said, "Yes, recommend me for ground school and I'll come Over There and help you win the war. I've got to go to ground school before they'll let me fly an airplane." He said, "What education have you got?" I said, "None." He said, "No college?" I said, "No." "No high school?" I said, "No." "Ever hear of algebra?" "No." "Ever hear of trigonometry?" "No." "Listen, that sixteen-week course is the toughest course in the United States. It's in Princeton, New Jersey—50 percent of our college graduates fail it. You wouldn't last as long as a snowball in hell." I said, "Colonel, I think you misunderstood me, I didn't ask you to get me through ground school, I asked you to get me in. If I can't get through that's my tough luck." He said, "Hell, I'll recommend you. What have I got to lose?"

Just a few days later I was in Princeton. Everyone there, a class of 160, everyone had a college degree. Everyone was asking, "What school are you from? What fraternity were you in?" I was a lone wolf. One of the boys walked over to me and said, "Benny, what school are you from?" I said, "Just the school of hard knocks." He said, "No, really." I said, "Really." Then I told him my story how I'd haunted recruiting stations and everything else—going into detail. Then he smiled and said, "You mean you went to all this trouble to get in this damn war?" I said, "Yes." He said, "And all I've been trying to do is stay out of the damn thing." I said, "Don't you want to fight?" He said, "Look, I don't want to fight." I said, "Then what are you doing here?" He said, "I just want to get those silver wings on my manly chest and hook the spurs on the top of my desk and let the maidens come and worship at the shrine." I thought that was sacrilegious. He said, "Hey, guys, come over here." They all came over. He said, "Tell them what you told me." So I started telling them dead earnest everything from start to finish. I'd see these college guys' looks of disbelief, and they'd wink. I paid no attention. I was in dead earnest so I just went on with my story until I got through.

Finally one guy said, "Tell you what let's do, let's get him through ground school and let him go Over There to win the damn war, and the rest of us won't have to go." I thought that was a good idea. The rest of them said, "I thought you said he didn't have any education." "He doesn't, but look, what did you major in?" "History." "You coach him in history." "What did you major in?" "Math." "You coach him in math." When I got through I had assigned to me a college major for every subject I had to take at Princeton. I wouldn't have lasted the first day. I didn't sleep for sixteen weeks. Every night one of them was beating me on the back, and when I woke up the next morning someone else beat me up. It became their project—get me through ground school. I was exhausted, but I'd rather die than not get through. Anyway, in sixteen weeks our class graduated and 50 percent of them failed. Those boys were not studying like I was and they didn't have the incentive I had. They were out having fun with the girls. I didn't have one date in sixteen weeks. I got out of there and got my wings.

I was assigned to the 198th Aero Squadron of the Signal Corps, U.S. Army, received my commission as an officer, and became a member of the "Flying Wildcats."

I was sent to Payhurst Field, Mineola Long Island, New York. I was assigned for overseas duty, fighter pilot. The day the Armistice was signed there was one guy not glad to see the war over. I wanted one week on the front.

Edna was my greatest champion. People would come to her once in a while and say, "Lloyd doesn't have any education." She'd say, "Don't you believe it. He graduated head of his class at Princeton."

MY FIRST WINGS—TWICE (BEGINNING ABOUT 1906)

When I was a boy, a teacher who used rouge and lipstick and wore form-fitting dresses came to teach in our school. Until then we had been looking at girls in rough clothes who worked in the fields, who were sunburned and windblown. They didn't have a chance against the "city model." In spite of the fact that our mothers and sisters warned us against painted ladies and about dresses and adornments that enhanced their beauty—all forbidden in the Bible—every little boy in the school fell in love with the teacher. We decided that we were going to marry her as soon as we grew up.

I would have to say in my case that, other than the schoolteacher, I was not really interested in girls. I didn't think they were exciting. I was getting a much bigger kick out of breaking broncos, bulldogging steers, and racing motorcycles. You must remember that we were little kids, sons and daughters of immigrants trying to eke out an existence in a new land—building homes and churches in a hard country. The towns were small settlements of a few hundred people, and we would probably get to town two or three times a year. So we were a long way from being sophisticated.

Then World War I became a reality. After many experiences I found myself at Princeton, New Jersey, going to ground school preparatory to learning to fly an airplane. Most people in our area had never even seen one, except in a picture. When we graduated and received our wings, I was among a graduating class of approximately sixty-five young men, sixty-four of them college graduates, and I who had never seen the inside of a high school and had very few months in the lower grades. We received our wings. Each of my buddies was sending his wings to his best girlfriend, then getting another pair for himself. I felt left out because I didn't really have a girlfriend. Then I thought of my schoolteacher! I told them I also was sending my wings to my best girlfriend (even though the girlfriend didn't know anything about how I felt). I bundled up my wings and mailed them. I got a lovely letter back. She bragged on what a fine young man I was and told me she would keep them always and would cherish them dearly because they had come from me. I went down and bought another pair of wings. When the war was over, I came back to Texas where I had taken my flight training. On a furlough in South Texas I met THE GIRL. I started going with her and when we became engaged, I gave her my wings and told her, "These were my first wings." I forgot entirely about the other pair I had mailed to my schoolteacher.

Many years later, when we were moving our furniture from one home to a new home we had built, these wings were somehow lost. We could never find them. Dolly and I were both very disappointed. After all, they were my first wings, and we had a lot of sentimental attachment to them. Many years after that I received a package in the mail. The address was in longhand, and it was easy to see the writing was that of an old person, grown quite feeble.

I opened the package. The message said, "This is your schoolteacher. I am quite frail, and the doctors tell me my time is short. I have always cherished these wings because they came from you. I never married. I guess because I fell in love with all the little boys that were my pupils. I have been thinking that I do not want anything as precious as these wings to fall into stranger's hands. They would not know the true story behind them. I am returning them so that you and I will always have them. Sincerely, Your Teacher."

Patrón

YOU CAN'T AFFORD TO BUY HER STOCKINGS (1918)

At the time I met this girl, she always seemed to have plenty of money (which she did until it was lost). She wore the loveliest clothes. I was so proud when I brought her to meet my folks. They, like everyone else, fell in love with her. Later, one day, my dad came to me and said, "Lloyd, you're spending a lot of time with Edna. Are you planning on marrying her?" I told him, "I sure am if I can talk her into it." He said, "Lloyd, that's what I want to talk to you about. Now don't misunderstand me. She is the prettiest, loveliest young lady. There isn't a man alive who wouldn't be proud and happy to have her as his wife, but, Lloyd, you've got no education. You're going to have to dig it out of the ground just like I did. I doubt if you could make a tenth of the money it would take to support her the way she was raised. Son, you can't afford to buy her stockings." I told him I had long since decided she was worth the effort and I'd find a way, come hell or high water.

OUT OF FAMILY AND OUT OF MONEY (1918)

When I met Dolly, I immediately fell in love with her. Pretty soon I was spending all my spare time having dates with her.

Dolly's grandparents on her mother's side were very wealthy ranchers from Texas and Montana. Her father's parents were Texas ranchers, but far from wealthy. When her mother's parents realized their daughter, Achsah Rebecca, a graduate of Southwestern in Georgetown, was becoming interested in a Texas cowboy, they made every effort to break the young couple up. The young couple, having minds of their own, eloped and married. A feud developed between the two families. Achsah sided with her young husband, Edward. A number of lawsuits were filed by the young husband against the wealthy ranchers. The feud became so bitter that they were not on speaking terms. Edna's mother died soon after Edna was born. The wealthy rancher came to Edna's grandmother on her father's side and said, "We have lost our daughter, and she was our only daughter. We are wealthy and can take Edna Ruth. She will be our daughter to us. She will enjoy the best of schools and colleges and the greatest luxuries and pleasures which you cannot possibly afford to give her." The grandmother, Catherine, replied, "We can appreciate the opportunities you can give Edna Ruth, but we can support her. She will grow up to be a fine young lady. If you take her, she might grow up to be like you, which I think is the worst thing that could happen to her."

Shortly afterward, the grandfather on her mother's side died and left Edna a sizeable inheritance. So as Edna grew up and commenced to want pretty clothes and luxuries that her grandmother could not afford, Catherine would say, "See your guardian. I'm sure he will let you have anything you want," which was true. Everyone in the little town where she lived knew that she was that little orphan girl that her grandmother was raising. She was so lovely and such a cute little tyke that when she went into the stores in the little town, they would give her candy and gum and presents. When she wanted pretty clothes and luxuries, she would go to her guardian, and he would give her a check to get them. So she grew up with the idea that everybody loved her, which was true, and loved to do things for her.

Shortly before I met Dolly, her grandmother Catherine died while nursing neighbors during the influenza epidemic. About the same time, her guardian had been playing the stock market with his own money and had gotten into trouble. Coming up short, in desperation he had used Edna's money to save his and lost that as well. So in a very short period of time Dolly found herself out of family and out of money. In spite of these financial reverses and the limited funds we had to live on when we were first married, I never heard her complain. We had been married only a short while when I realized two things. One was that the honeymoon would never end. The other was that if I worked hard enough, I could do a lot of things that made her happy. In short, she virtually spent her life seeing what she could do to make me happy, and I, in turn, spent my life seeing what I could do to make her happy. It worked. Instead of the honeymoon ending, it grew more precious by the year.

WE DON'T WANT ANY PAY (1920)

The war ended, and I came back to Mission, Texas. Within a year Dolly and I were married. I had no money—in fact, I think I had a dollar and a half. I went to the bank in Mission, told them who I was and that I intended to live in this country. I talked them into loaning me $500! We moved into a little house by the side of the Edinburg canal. There was no honeymoon.

Two people could not have been more mismatched. I had gone to school very little, and, being an immigrant's son, I had worked from the time I could walk. At thirteen I began following the harvest around the country. Contrary to that, Dolly's mother had died in childbirth, and her grandmother had reared her. She had been left considerable money by her grandfather on her mother's side. This was in charge of a guardian (and later lost by that guardian). Her grandmother thought that with this kind of money, she should live like a lady and not soil her hands with work. So the lovely girl I married had never cooked a meal, never swept a floor, never made a bed. She spent her time in Sunday school and church, as an old-fashioned Baptist grandmother would insist upon. She was quite athletic and played basketball all through the school year.

When we moved into that little house on the side of the Edinburg canal, I was sure I would have to go into the kitchen to show her how to cook bacon and eggs. But that first morning, two little Mexican girls, the same age as Dolly, came to the house and said in Spanish, "We're the canal rider's daughters that live in the brush on the other side of the canal, and we want to work for you." Dolly said, "I'm sorry, but I don't have the money to pay for anything." Their reply was, "We don't want any pay. You're so pretty, we just want to work for you." She said, "Come right in." Lupe and Consuelo cooked our first meal in that little house and stayed thirty-seven years. I used to tease Dolly that she must have lost her looks because I remember we had to start paying them by the week. The third girl came to the house and had about the same conversation two weeks later. Luz stayed fifty-two years. The three girls simply became a part of our family. They learned to speak a little English, and my Dolly learned a little Spanish. They got along great.

ALL GOOD SHOTS (1920)

I was married in 1920. That same year, on November 11, we had our first American Legion celebration in the Valley. It was held at the baseball diamond west of Mission. At least five hundred ex-servicemen attended, and it was a great party. My brother Elmer and I both went. The times we had had in the service were so recent that it was no problem for all these ex-servicemen to fall back into the pattern. Everyone was drinking, eating barbecue, and having a lot of fun. As the night wore on and the drinking increased, there were more and more fights. I had one, and Elmer apparently enjoyed it more—he had three.

A man who said he was running for railroad commissioner got up on a table to make a speech. I jerked him off the table because I didn't think our celebration should be marred by speechmaking.

As the twilight faded a young man was walking around on the baseball diamond shooting a rifle at pebbles that lay along the ground. I walked up to him and asked. "Can you shoot that thing?" He said, "You bet your life I can shoot this thing!" I picked up a half-pint whiskey bottle that had been emptied and held it out in my hand for him to shoot. Some men who saw what was going on began to yell "Cut that out! We won't have it!"

We paid no attention. He fired and missed the bottle. I told him that was as bad shootin' as I had seen recently. I set the bottle on my head and asked, "Can you hit it now?" I remember hearing men call out again, "Cut that out!" We will not have that!" Again we paid no attention, and he leveled the rifle at my head so that when I looked up at the sights, I realized he had taken dead aim at my forehead. I remember wondering if he was really that drunk or was just playing. I was very happy to see him raise the rifle. He aimed again, and the glass fell down around my shoulders. The next year firearms were barred from the celebration.

This party lasted all night. The next morning found everyone feeling much the worse for the wear and heading home. I got out of the car that brought me home, suffering a little remorse because instead of acting like a respectable married man, I had been anything but—all night long. I expected to hear from my lovely wife, if and when she ever found out what had gone on.

As I stepped up to the door, it opened. She was standing waiting for me. She threw her arms around me and gave me a big hug and kiss, then asked, "Did you have a good time?" I answered, "Yes, Darlin', maybe too much of a good time." She smiled, "I heard about it." "How did you hear about it," I asked. She said that some of the boys had told Mildred Baker, who was one of her closest friends. Mildred had called Dolly and told her all about it. "And what did you tell Mildred Baker?" I asked. "Well, I told her I thought that the boys who had been in the service so long and were just now getting home and settling down should be entitled to celebrate one night." I said, "Bless your heart, Dolly. I'm sorry about what happened, but maybe it's not a total loss. I've decided to tell you now, I'm through drinking." She said, "Do you really mean it?" I answered, "Yes, I really mean it." Then she said, "I'm so happy." That was the last wild celebration, and I kept my commitment.

The aftermath of this story . . . a large crowd was present when the sugar mill in the Valley was dedicated by Lloyd Jr. Dolly and I were among the guests, and because we were the senator's mother and dad, we were on the speaker's platform. After the dedication was over, a man about my age, tall and slender, walked up to me, stuck out his hand and said, "Hello, Lloyd." I said, "Am I supposed to know you?" His reply was, "How many men have you had shoot a bottle off your head?" My God, I was sure glad to see him! I had not seen the shooter for at least fifty years and, although there had been others, I remembered him so well because he was the last one who had done it. Now, as I look back through the years, I am thankful they were all good shots!

CREDIT CARDS

I began growing vegetables and hit a very good year. I was a little money ahead. Then I began clearing land. In those days it was customary for the land companies to pay $15 an acre for clearing directly to the contractor. There was no control of the U.S.–Mexico border then, and people came and went as they liked. Things were very bad on the other side. People were hungry. It was bad here, too, but there was work. They came across by the hundreds. I noticed the contractors were paying the workers who cleared the brush $7.50 an acre. Men, women, and children all worked to eke out an existence. I decided that maybe this was a business I could get into, so I went to a wholesale house and told them I wanted to go into the land-clearing business. My plan was that I would need to buy groceries and supplies on thirty-days time. I sold them on the idea. They agreed, and, if my bill was paid, they would go another thirty days, etc. I took a large barn that was on the property I was renting and converted it into a commissary.

I went to the land companies and asked if they would give me contracts for clearing the brush at $15 an acre. They said they would because they weren't getting very good service from the people they were dealing with. Then I went to the jefes of the workers doing the clearing. Each group had its own jefe who did their talking and measuring. When I told them I'd like to have them work for me, their first question was, "Do you have any money?" My answer was, "No, I don't." They asked, "Why should we work for you?" My reply was, "A very good reason—you'll make more money." I explained to them what I had in mind. If the land company paid me $15 an acre for the land we cleared, I was going to pay them the full $15. They were skeptical. "The deal's not honest. Nobody works for nothing!" I told them it was honest, and I would explain it.

I told them that the way they were working now, when the land company paid the contractor $15, he gave them $7.50 of it. They took the $7.50, went to the store, and bought their groceries and supplies, but the storekeeper had a 25 percent mark-up on what he was selling them. So, in reality, they were getting only 37½ cents out of every dollar that was paid for clearing. What I intended to do was give them the full $15, but give it to them in a "credit card" that was good in my commissary, where I would have the same prices they had in town. So I would be making the storekeeper's profit, and they would be going home with 75 cents out of every dollar instead of 37½ cents—or, in reality—twice as many groceries and supplies as they were getting now. I think I was probably the first to offer credit cards, at least in this part of Texas.

We had cards printed up that had nickels, dimes, quarters, halves, and dollars, and there were $5, $10, $25, and $50 credit cards. The young lady that operated my commissary had a little punch. She would figure their bills and show them what she was going to punch out of their card. I told them not to lose their cards because they were the same as money. This worked fine. Word got around that those who worked for me got twice as much as anyone else. It wasn't long until it looked like I was doing practically all the land clearing in the entire area. I would fill my commissary on Monday morning, and it would be empty by Saturday night—at the 25 percent markup. I began making real money for the first time in my life.

THE BABY BLUE DRESS

Up to this time, I had not bought my lovely wife any new clothes. Being rather inexperienced (because this was the first wife I ever had) and because she had so many clothes left over from the days with her grandmother and her guardian, I didn't realize she was wearing out the last of the clothes she had. It was inevitable that one day she would come to me and say, "Lloyd, I was invited to a party, and I don't have anything to wear." I said, "Well, Dolly, I'm making money now, and we have this new Ford car [which cost a total sum of $485, brand new with all the accessories]. Why don't we go to San Antonio? We can call it our honeymoon, and we'll buy you a new dress?" She said she would love it, so, without any hesitation, we got in the car and headed for San Antonio.

South of Falfurrias, we came to the sand. People were stopped by the roadside, pumping up their tires. They told us we would have to let about half the air out of our tires so they would widen out a little. In this manner we could cross the sand without getting stuck if we moved rapidly. On the other side of the sand we would have to take a hand pump and pump the tires back up to pressure. It took about two hours to pump up the four tires. In those days, those tires carried ninety-pound pressure. It was all dirt road with deep ruts, and our trip to San Antonio took seventeen hours.

We got to San Antonio, went to the Menger Hotel, and I was shocked to see what a room was going to cost us. Up to that time, when I was with the laborers working with the harvest, we never paid in excess of twenty cents for an overnight room for three or four of us in the same room. Anyway, the next morning we walked down to a store she had traded in many times with her grandmother, and I told her, "Now, Dolly, I don't believe I brought enough money because we left so quick, and I don't have any money in the bank, but I have a lot of money coming from the land companies for clearing that we've already done. So you give them a check for anything you want and let me know how much it is. When we get home, I'll draw the money on the clearing and put it in the bank. It will take three or four days by mail for your check to clear the bank, so your check will be good." She said, "They'll take the check because they know me. I've been there so often with Grandmother."

In those days, you could buy a nice dress for $3 or $4, $10 would have been the top. Because I was so proud of my lovely wife, I wanted her to wear the finest clothes. I expected to have to pay maybe even $10 for the dress. When we came into the store and went to the dress department, a lady who knew Dolly grabbed her by the hand and said, "I have something to show you." My Dolly was an extreme blonde, and, in a few minutes, she came out in what I thought was the loveliest dress I had ever seen in my life. It was baby blue, close to the color of her eyes, and form fitting. She spun around and said, "Lloyd, I love it and I want it." I said, "Dolly, it's the most beautiful dress I have ever seen, and you have got to have it. How much is it?" The reply was $67.50." I caught my breath and said, "Well, I don't care. You give them a check for it and I will get it covered."

She went back with the lady and in a few minutes came out with a little hat on the side of her head and a new pair of slippers. She said, "Lloyd, I have got to have the hat and the pumps to go with the dress." I was still numb from the $67.50, and I said, "Okay, Dolly, give them a check for all of it." She was happy, and so was I. But I was still thinking about the $67.50 the dress cost and thought I could reduce the hotel bill some by getting started early and driving all night. I told Dolly she could sleep in the car while I drove. Since the trip coming up had taken seventeen hours, I presumed it would take the same time going home. It would have except that when we got to the sand, because there was dew on the sand, we didn't have to let so much air out of the tires.

She slept on my shoulder nearly all night. I had been driving at about fifteen miles an hour, thinking about the $67.50. I had noticed on the hat a little spot of mink not much bigger than a dot. I had run a trap line as a boy in South Dakota and had trapped and sold pelts for $1 or $2—$5 for the best—so I knew this little spot of mink could not possibly be worth more than twenty-five cents.

Anyway, we were nearly home when she woke up. I turned to my lovely wife and said, "Dolly, how much was the check you gave them in the store?" Her reply was, "Well, Lloyd, I don't know." "Dolly, don't ever sign a check unless you look at it and see that the check is right." She said, "Lloyd, they wouldn't steal anything." My reply was, "I didn't say they would steal anything, but how do I know how much to put in the bank unless I know how much the check was? Now the dress was $67.50. How much were the hat and the pumps?" She said, "I think $125, the hat was the most expensive."

What she said shocked me because money was that scarce. "Dolly, I told you I didn't have any money in the bank." She smiled real sweetly and said, "That's it. That's why I did it." We were driving very slowly, and I said, "Dolly, I don't understand. Are you telling me that if I had the money in the bank you might not have done this, but because I didn't have the money in the bank you did?" She didn't say yes or no. She just moved a little closer and said, "Darling, it shows the confidence I have in you, and you want me to have confidence in you, don't you?" And I told her, "Yes, Darling, I do want you to have confidence in me."

CHOKE, DON'T SHOOT (1921)

I began renting land and growing cotton. It was important to get my cotton out before a storm damaged it, and I was heavily in debt. I took a load of cotton to Mission and told Taylor at the gin that while I was away, someone had moved in with two big trucks and hauled all my pickers to Mississippi. I didn't know where I could get any more pickers.

Another man standing by heard the conversation. He introduced himself and told me he knew there was a local man working for the Mississippi people who was getting $1 a head for all the labor he could steal from us and load on their trucks. He said, "There he is now! Why don't you beat hell out of him?"

I was desperate and told him I was going to put a stop to it. I didn't know there was bad blood between the man doing the accusing and the accused.

I walked out to meet the accused. He was about forty years old and had a heavy pistol hanging on his right hip. Knowing that an argument might be unpleasant, I didn't want him to be able to get hold of his gun too easily. So I walked up to him, put out my right hand and introduced myself. He took hold of my hand. I made certain I didn't let loose of his right hand while I told him I understood that he was stealing help from the cotton growers in the Valley and that he was selling the Valley growers out by turning our help to the group from Mississippi for $1 a head.

He became furious and tried to pull his hand loose. When he realized I wasn't going to let him go, he said, "You're a stranger here or you wouldn't be talkin' like that 'cause if you weren't a stranger and if you did, I'd shoot your damn guts out." I answered, "Drop your gun. We'll settle it right here." But he went on, "You're new here; you don't comprende. Somebody put you up to this because they hate me. I'm not asking you to believe me, but I don't apologize for anything I do. I'll tell you what I will do. You get the man who accused me of this job, and I'll either get him up on the public square to admit he's a damn liar or I'll cut his guts out." This man I was talking to, I learned later, was from a family that had moved to the Valley and were responsible for several gunfights where opponents had been killed. One or two of the family members had been wounded in these shooting scrapes.

I told him to wait where he was, released his hand, and told him I'd bring the man to face him. I went back to the gin and told the accuser to come and tell him to his face. He said, "No, he'll kill me, and you, too, with that damn gun. And if you tell him I'm the man who told you, I'll deny it. He'll kill me!" Disgusted, I went back and told the fellow his accuser was yellow and wouldn't face him. He said, "I know who the S.O.B. is. I could have told you he wouldn't face me."

The result of it was that I told him our problem and he said he'd like to go to work for me, keeping our labor here. I hired him on the spot, and we began working together picking up labor as they crossed the river, hiring them, and hauling them to our fields.

I soon realized that the Mississippi group was continuing to steal our workers. So we decided it was time for a showdown. We caught two of their men on the river. This fellow and I, along with my brother Elmer took them forcibly, after an argument, and put them in our car. They became very frightened.

We took them down alongside the river. This fellow and Elmer were talking loud enough so the two guys could hear them. They were trying to decide what to do with their bodies after we killed them. I was taking the attitude, in their presence, that we shouldn't kill them, but Elmer and this other fellow were very positive in overriding my objections. Finally, we stopped on the bank of the Rio Grande. They insisted these guys be shot and thrown in the river. I pointed out to them that when they were found, the bodies would show they had been shot—better to choke them to death and throw them in the river. There would be no serious evidence that they had been manhandled.

The two guys knew I was the only friend they had! After an hour and a half of pleading, very much opposed by Elmer and my friend, I finally insisted they be allowed to go back to Mississippi. But if they ever showed up again and we caught them, I wouldn't stand in the way of doing what they thought should be done with these two rascals.

Needless to say, we never saw them again. And we three had a good laugh.

"I WILL KILL YOU" (1922)

A neighbor of mine came to see me one morning and told me his wife was ill and he had to take her to the hospital. He had some water coming for a cabbage patch and wondered if I could take a couple of men to look after the irrigation for him until he got back.

I was farming thousands of acres and, of course, had a lot of men working for me. So I took two of the men in my car, drove over to the cabbage patch, told the men what I wanted, and showed them where the gate was.

As I got ready to leave, I turned to the two men and realized one of them was a man I had never seen before. This was not too unusual since I had so many men. I told this new man that I had so many heads of water running that I might be a little late relieving him the next morning. (They were to irrigate all night.) I said, "I will be here as near seven in the morning as I can, but, if I'm an hour or so late, you'll be paid for the extra time. But take care of the water until I get here. This man is a good friend of mine, and I want to do him a good job."

This new man said, "You be here at seven in the morning." This surprised me a little, but I said, "I will be here as near seven as I can, but you take care of it until I get here. You'll be paid extra." He repeated exactly what he had said before. I realized he was trying to pick a quarrel with me, but I always did everything I could to avoid problems, so I ignored what he said and left, still very much irritated by his attitude. I decided that after this irrigation job was finished, I'd let him go. I did not need people who were looking for trouble.

The next morning I had so many men to distribute I was about forty-five minutes late. When I got there, many of the borders were broken and water was running everywhere. The man had quit looking after the water at least two hours earlier. What had happened could not have happened in the forty-five minutes that I was late. I was furious. I told the new man that they had quit looking after the irrigating two or three hours earlier, and that I didn't have any more work for him.

I was standing quite close to him when I made the remark and he cursed me. I struck him across the mouth with the back of my hand. He threw as pretty a right cross as I had seen in a long time, which, fortunately, I was able to block with my shoulder. I realized this whole plan had been intentional. I had a real fight on my hands—this man had had some training. I was thankful I, too, had had considerable training. In a few moments he realized he'd made a mistake. Since he had deliberately picked the fight, I proceeded to give him a boxing lesson and then knocked him down. He said, "You have made a big mistake, and I will kill you." I was furious. I told him I heard what he said, but I had been threatened so many times, that one more didn't make any difference. He screamed, "Es diferente."

We had two girls working in our home. They would alternate Sundays visiting their folks, who lived south of Mission. The following Sunday night we were driving to bring Lupe home from her visit. We drove over a high canal that had a wooden bridge over it. It was just turning dusk in the evening. I was driving with Dolly beside me in the front seat. Lloyd Jr. was a baby and was lying in the back seat. There was a crash! Pieces of the front window fell into the car. I stopped the car. There was a bullet hole in the right front window. I saw Dolly was not hurt. We both whirled around to look at Lloyd Jr. There was a little blood on his forehead, and there was another hole in the left rear window. Someone had fired a bullet at our car. It had entered the front window on the right side and glanced in front of Dolly's face, back of my head, and through the left rear window. The shattered pieces of glass, or at least one of them, had hit Lloyd Jr. on the forehead. It was bleeding. From then on he carried a scar from it. I realized then that this had been a deliberate attempt to really hurt me and my family. I immediately gave gas to the car and drove fast for half a mile without lights. I was driving with my left hand and holding Dolly with my right arm. She was screaming that Lloyd Jr. had been hurt.

When I felt we were out of range, we took stock of what had happened and realized no one was seriously hurt. Needless to say, I associated the incident with the man I had had the disagreement with earlier in the week.

The next morning I talked to a number of my men, not telling them what had happened, but asking them where the troublemaker lived. They said, yes, he lived with a widow woman and two grown sons in a little settlement called Ojo de Agua. I didn't want any trouble, but I would not run, and neither could I permit someone to shoot through my car with my family in it. There had to be a showdown.

The following morning I got up at four. It was quite cold, so I put on a heavy Mackinaw. This was before we had electric lights, so I lit an Aladdin lamp. Dolly wanted to know where I was going. I told her I thought I knew where the man who shot through our car lived, and I was going to find him.

She begged me not to have any trouble. I told her I didn't want trouble either, but I had to find him before he took another shot from ambush. We might not be lucky the next time.

I took a .45-caliber pistol, put it in my pocket, and headed for Ojo de Agua. When I got there, I picked out the house my men had described to me. I had my right hand in my Mackinaw pocket, with the .45 aimed forward so I could shoot through the pocket. My finger was on the trigger. I knocked on the door with my left hand. There was no sound from inside. I knocked louder the second time with the same result. I stepped back and drove my right foot into the door where the latch was, and the door flew open. I still had my finger on the trigger of the .45. The small house was lived-in all right, but there was nobody there. I was sure my "friend" was in one of the other houses watching me, but I couldn't search all the houses, so I went back home.

The next morning I followed the same procedure. The door had been repaired. I knocked on the door and when there was no answer, I kicked it from the hinges and found once again there was no one inside. I got into my car and went home, knowing sooner or later I would find him.

The following afternoon a constable in Mission stopped me as I was driving through town and told me he would like to talk to me. I said, "All right." He asked what I was going to do when I found the man I was looking for. I told him I had no choice. I would shoot him. I couldn't afford to let him run around loose when he would shoot through my car from ambush. He asked if I would be willing to forget the entire incident if he could get the other party to do likewise. I told him, "Probably not." If I ever saw that fellow again, I would either have to kill him or live in constant fear that he might injure my family. Then he asked if I would be willing to talk to the fellow. I told him that if the fellow wanted to talk to me, the only chance he had was to come to my house, unarmed. The constable asked, "What would you do?" I answered, "Probably shoot him." He said, "He doesn't have much of a chance, does he?" My reply was that he didn't deserve a chance.

The next morning I got up again about four and lit the Aladdin lamp. When I opened the back door, in the bright light, I saw a man standing there with his hands high over his head. I jerked the pistol from my pocket. He fell to his knees saying, "Please, please, please." I said, "You S.O.B., I ought to kill you." He said, "If you don't, I'll be your friend as long as you live." I answered, "Not as long as I live, but as long as you live, and you don't have much chance of living."

But I did talk with him a little while. He told me that he would never have gotten into the mess, but that he had started living with a widow woman who had two grown sons that I had fired a couple of weeks before. When they found out that he had some pugilistic experience, they wanted the satisfaction of having him beat me up. He had foolishly gone along with the idea. Then, when I had gotten the best of him in the fight, they had got him to drinking and made him promise to eliminate me. After this talk, I decided to let him go.

Over the following years when I would go duck hunting near Ojo de Agua, my friend would hear the shooting, come down to shake my hand, and always remind me what good friends we really were.

A REAL GOOD SELLING JOB (1924)

In our farming operation we had a thirty-eight-acre tract located at Hidalgo, Texas. I had sent a tractor down there to plow the tract. The following forenoon I received word that the tractor was broken down, so I drove to Hidalgo and found the tractor. The driver had let it run out of oil and had burned the bearings. There was no excuse for what he had done because he was told to check the oil and fuel in the morning and at noon of each day. I fired him. He became very abusive. We wound up in a fight, which he quickly learned he should not have started. As he left, he said that he would get even with me and that he would see that I didn't live if I stayed around Hidalgo, Texas. I told him I had heard that kind of threat so many times that one more time didn't make any difference. He answered that I would find out to my sorrow. Anyway, that night I got another man to help me. We went down and started to overhaul the tractor by the lights of our car. Along about eleven o'clock, I thought I heard a click at some distance away from us. The man who was helping me asked if I had heard anything. I answered, "Yes, it sounded like a lever-action rifle where you reject an empty shell and install a loaded shell in the barrel." He said he thought the same thing.

We sat there a while and finally decided that we had just imagined we heard something, even though there was a thick clump of trees growing along the canal bank about two hundred yards away. We turned the car lights back on and began again to overhaul the tractor.

The next thing we heard was the whine of a bullet as it passed near the tractor. My man jumped down from the tractor and said, "That's the S.O.B. you fired today." I answered, "José, if that's true, he has to be in those trees on the canal bank and that's close enough that if he really wanted to, he could have hit either one of us. It shows he doesn't want to kill anybody. He just wants to scare us away from the tractor. That's not serious shooting." He said, "Por cierto, I'm not going to stand up there while he's out in the brush." So I climbed up on the tractor and began trying to finish the job. As soon as I started working, the next bullet was so close to my head that I felt it fan my cheek. This time he had done a real good selling job.

I jumped down to the car, snapped out the lights, and drove without lights for about three-quarters of a mile across rough ground until I reached the road. I decided he was firing the first bullet hoping to get us separated, and the second bullet was meant for me. José and I knew who the fellow was, but I had no gun. We weren't going to hunt him in the dark when he could be hiding in ambush.

We did check out the brush the next day and found no evidence of where he had been. We finished the overhauling of the tractor motor in the daylight. We never saw that man again.

MORTGAGED MULES (1924)

I began to expand my farming and land clearing operation with damn little money. I figured out a procedure.

One of the farmers I was financing was Higinio Ramirez. I had bought some land, which the bank had financed for me. I figured Higinio and his family could farm three hundred acres of irrigated land, so I sold him a pair of mules and some machinery and took a mortgage on them and on the crop. I traded this note, with my endorsement on it, to the bank, picking up my own note so I would not be above the bank's $5,000 line of credit per person.

A few days after I had delivered the mules and machinery to Higinio, and had his note in the bank and the mortgage, of course, filed of record, Higinio came to my headquarters. He said, "I have lost my mules." When I asked him how, he told me that formerly he had rented a farm from the county sheriff. When they had a drought and the river was out of water for irrigation, he was unable to pay the sheriff. Since the sheriff refused to finance him, he had to move.

Apparently, the sheriff had learned that Higinio was farming with me and that he had some mules and machinery. The sheriff had come out with another man and taken the mules to his corrals. I asked Higinio if he knew where the sheriff's corrals were, and he answered, "Yes." We got in my car and he asked, "What are we going to do?" I said, "We're going to get our mules." He was scared. He said he wouldn't go because the sheriff would shoot at us. I threatened him enough that he got in my old jalopy and directed me. We drove up to the corrals. There was nobody there. Then we went looking for our mules. Along with several other mules, there were the mules with my brand that I had sold to Higinio. We opened the gate, went in with our rope, roped the mules, and Higinio, sitting in the back seat of my jalopy, led the mules while I drove slowly back to our corrals. This was early in the morning.

About two in the afternoon, a car drove in my yard. I saw his sheriff's badge on his vest. I introduced myself, but he didn't acknowledge the introduction. He simply said, "Did you pick up some mules out of my corral on the Retama Tract?" I answered, "Yes, and they're out in my corral right there." He said, "I'll give you two hours to have them back in my corral." I said, "Sheriff, I'm sorry, but I don't want you to give me anything, so I'll just give you those two hours back. Those mules were my property, and I sold them to Higinio Ramirez. I took a mortgage on them at the time I sold them and the mortgage is of record and is held by the First National Bank of Mission." His next remark was, "If you had any claim on those mules, you have due process of law. You get them back in my corral like I told you—within two hours—then you can go to court to prove your case." My reply was, "Sheriff, I'm sorry, but you didn't follow due process of law when you took them out of my corral. Because of that, I have possession now and I intend to keep them." He warned me, "I'll send a deputy within an hour. He'll take them by force." I said, "I'm sorry, Sheriff, but I told you I don't intend to give them up. They are my property and I am going to protect them. I have an automatic rifle in my house. If you send somebody out here, you'd better send somebody you don't like, because if he tries to take those mules out of my corral, he will be lying right there in the corral with them." The sheriff said, "The deputy will be here in an hour." I warned him, "You remember what I told you, because I meant it."

The sheriff continued to argue: "You're new here and if you don't like this country down here, why don't you leave?" I replied, "I like the country down here. I have a wife and a baby in the house. I intend to stay. I think we just got through fighting a war, and I think it was in defense of our rights. If I have to fight a second one here, then this is where it will begin." He drove off, and the deputy never came and got the mules.

HEAD HIM OFF (1924)

Dolly and I were living in a little house completely surrounded by brush. My workers and I were farming a lot of land and clearing brush. The conditions were primitive. Families had put up shelters of any kind they could. Among them was a man called Macrecio, his wife, and their son, José. The wife was a tireless worker—they all were—but Macrecio himself was pretty much a brute while she was a delicate little woman, very subservient. She lived for one purpose and that was to be a servant to Macrecio, always trying to please him, and to take care of José, who was a big boy but quite handicapped mentally. They lived only fifty yards from our home in a pretty good shelter they had established under a mesquite tree. The shelter was divided into a kitchen and a combined bedroom and living room. It was open to the south, and it had a tin and reed roof. The reed walls were held together with sticks.

Macrecio had a vile temper. We would often hear screaming. I would run out there to find Macrecio unmercifully beating his wife. I would separate them and threaten to call the Rangers to pick him up and throw him in jail. Regardless, it continued, and happened many, many times.

One day there was a great deal of screaming—by both Macrecio's wife and his son. José was trying to stop the beating. He was a big boy for his twelve or thirteen years. I ran to their house. The wife was lying on the floor. Macrecio had one foot on her arm, holding her down. He had pulled a bed slat out from under the mattress and was beating her with the bed slat with one hand while he held José off with the other. As I came into range, I struck him a terrific blow on the side of the head and knocked him down, but not out. He leaped to his feet and threatened to kill me. As mad as he was, I knew at that time that he meant it, but I ignored him and then threatened him with what I would do if he ever beat his wife again. I left. Back at my house I told Dolly what had happened. She was shocked because Macrecio's wife was a sweet woman and did everything that was possible to please her husband.

I had a nice garden and about fifteen young shoats in a small pen, figuring all of this was necessary to eke out an existence for my wife and baby. Times were very hard, and I would throw as much feed as I could gather to these shoats. Of course, it was never enough, so when I'd get to the edge of the fence, they would come squealing for more food. I didn't have more food or the money to buy more. This caused them to dig under the fence once in a while and get out and do a lot of damage in the garden, munching potatoes, carrots, and anything else they could eat.

After my run-in with Macrecio, I was furious with him. I went down to my pigpen and saw the pig in the garden and the hole in the fence. I figured that if I went in after the pig, he would head for the hole and get back through the fence to the pigpen. Then I could repair the fence. But when I ran around him he ran back to the fence, didn't want to go through the hole, and ran past it almost to Macrecio's house. So I opened the gate, which was closed, to his house, and called to Macrecio in Spanish, "I'm going to run the pig and head him back to the gate. Hold out your hands when the pig is close to the opening and he'll run through the open gate." He had his arms folded and just glowered at me. He didn't say yes or no. "Macrecio," I said, "head him off!" He never said a word. I was getting madder by the minute. I ran around the pig the other way and brought him back again past the gate on a dead run. I yelled at Macrecio, "Head him off!" He simply stood there and never moved his hand. Naturally, the pig ran by the open gate. I was ready to explode but said as quietly as I could as I ran by Macrecio, "Next time he comes around, you had better head him off." His reply, with a curse word, was, "Head him off yourself!" By that time, I was madder at Macrecio than I was at the pig. I brought the pig back by the open gate on a dead run and screamed at Macrecio, "Head him off!" He cursed and said something I didn't understand. The pig ran by the open gate. I grabbed Macrecio as I went by and wrapped a little bullwhip around both his legs. He told me, "Voy por mi escopeta y terminamos."

A short distance from his house, his two sons-in-law were staying. They usually kept their single-shot shotgun to shoot rattlesnakes and rabbits to eat. When I saw him run for their house, I knew he was after the shotgun. Still watching, I worked around to my house, intending to get my gun.

When Macrecio got to the sons-in-law's place he found out someone about half a mile away had borrowed the single-shot shotgun. There was an old horse, probably thirty years old, starved and weak, tied to a mesquite tree. Macrecio hitched this horse to an old rattletrap buckboard that they had, climbed up on the buckboard and hollered at the horse. The horse moved a little, pulled the buckboard about two feet, and stopped. There was no whip in the buckboard, so Macrecio grabbed the ax from the woodpile. (Everyone had an ax in those days.) He took that ax to use as a whip, and, screaming at the old horse, turned the handle of the ax and hit him over the backbone, which was nothing but skin and bones. The horse shuffled three or four steps and slowed down. Then Macrecio would hit him again, determined to go get the shotgun.

I watched for him the rest of the afternoon, but he didn't show. That evening when I came into the house, I told Dolly to pull the curtains and keep them down because there was no telling what Macrecio might do. I didn't want him shooting through the windows after dark.

The little house we lived in was built so that our bedroom extended about six feet beyond the other south line of the house. There was a window on the extended part of the house by our bedroom.

In the morning when I woke up, it was just turning daybreak. I pulled the shade aside and looked out the window. There was Macrecio sitting about twenty feet from that window on a log about eight inches high and probably six inches across, his side toward the window. He was looking around the corner of the house where I always came out in the morning to assign jobs to my men. Across his legs was the single-shot shotgun. I slipped out of bed, reached under the shade, and eased the window open. I had a 12-gauge standing by the side of our bed. I picked up the shotgun, carefully shoved it out the window, and aimed it at the log he was sitting on, still with his side toward me. I squeezed off the trigger, not caring if a few shots might have stung him a little as the rest of the shots hit the log he was sitting on.

At that close range the blast was tremendous. It completely knocked the log out from under him so that he fell over backward with his gun pointing straight into the air, and it exploded! Because the charge was so close and such a loud racket, I am sure he thought he had been shot! He rolled over on his hands and feet but did not take time to straighten up. He ran on his hands and feet like a big spider before finally realizing he could straighten up. He left his shotgun when he ran into the brush. I went out and retrieved it and took it into the house for safety's sake.

I did not see Macrecio any more that day, but always kept my eyes open for him. The next morning I cautiously came out the kitchen door, watching for him. I had kept his shotgun. I saw all my men lined up for their instructions. Way to the back of the group was Macrecio, his jaw sticking out about a foot, but not saying a word. I allocated work to all the men except Macrecio and then walked out of the house, past the men, and proceeded to do other things that were necessary before I left the place. After the men left, he was following behind me as I did the other work. I was careful to see that he didn't get too close. After following me for about five minutes, he said, "Mr. Lloyd." I didn't answer him. I had made up my mind I was going to make him wait. Finally, I turned around and said, "Macrecio, what do you want?" He answered, "Quiero trabajar." I asked him, "If I put you back to work, will you stop beating your wife and follow my orders? If you won't, I don't want you on my place." His answer was, "Como usted dice." I put him back to work.

The climax of this story is that sometime after that, I told Macrecio I couldn't give him any more work because of the way he treated his wife and José. They moved away. A few weeks after that, some constables came by my house and told me that Macrecio had been beating his wife when José interfered, and Macrecio had grabbed the ax and split José's skull, killing him. I asked what they had done with Macrecio. They said, "He's dead." They had shot him.

FAR ENOUGH AWAY FROM THE BEST PATRÓN (1924)

Clearing the brush in this country, our work force grew very rapidly. The same growth applied to our farming operation. Most of our workers were honest, efficient, good and hard-working people, but, like humans everywhere, they had some peculiar traits.

While I came here not knowing a word of Spanish, I would soon be working hundreds of men, using their language. My rendition was not educated, but it was rapid. It was Border Spanish. You did everything you could to get along, but you had to be the boss and have the final answer or it didn't work.

One of the men I will always remember was a man called Paredes Ballí. This man was a widower with two little children he called Fale and Beak. I don't know where the names came from or why. This man was faithful, a tireless worker. In chopping cotton or any other work, he would make it a rule to work harder and faster than any other man I had in the organization. He had one weakness—he had to get drunk every Saturday night. He had a ritual he would follow. After he had been drinking on Saturday night, he would come up to me and, thumping his chest as if for emphasis, say, "Yo soy Paredes Ballí. Usted es mi patrón. Mi crédito es bueno con mi patrón, sí?" I would answer back, "Sí, su credito es bueno con su patrón." He would then say, "Présteme cinco dólares." I would give him the five dollars and, in those days, five dollars was a lot of money. A half dozen of his buddies would go with him until they drank up his five dollars. This had gone on for several weeks.

One Monday morning he came up to me—our communication was always in Spanish—and said, "I need to talk to you, very serious." I replied, "Yes, Paredes, what's the problem?" He said, "Do you pay me the same wages you pay all the other men?" I said, "Yes, Paredes. Every man gets one dollar a day and one dollar a night. You work steady, you draw the same rate as any other man, and you make good money." Then he said, "If this is true, and you say it is, then why is it my little Fale and Beak have such shabby clothes and never have any shoes?" I said, "Paredes, the trouble is that each Saturday when I pay everyone, you have been drinking. You come up to me and ask me to loan you five dollars, which you and your buddies drink up. So you have very little money left, only two or three dollars, if you've worked a full seven days." He asked, "Why do you loan me the money when I am drinking and when you know those friends are not really my friends except to drink up my liquor?"

I told him, "Paredes, I loan it to you because you are a good man, and you ask me to loan it to you." "Patrón," he said, "the next time I ask you to loan me money, you tell me, 'No.' In front of these people tell me they are not my friends and are just drinking my liquor." I said, "Paredes, I can do that, but how do I know that when I tell you that in front of them, that it won't make you mad, then we'll have trouble?" He said, "It doesn't make any difference. You do what I ask and don't loan me the money." I said, "All right, I will."

The next Saturday he approached me with his half-dozen hangers-on and went through the same routine. To avoid trouble, I said very close to him, "Paredes, you are one of my best men. Your credit is always good with me, but you asked me last week not to loan you any more money when you were drinking because your false friends were drinking it up and preventing you from buying nice clothes for Fale and Beak." He became furious and commenced to scream, threw his hat on the ground and stomped it. "I am nobody! I have no credit! My patrón won't loan me a dime." It was quite a scene. He was almost hysterical, or acted so, and I couldn't get a word in edgewise, so I went on home. His buddies, of course, were laughing and ridiculing him.

I was feeling bad about it because he was such a great fellow otherwise, and so loyal. I had just come in the house for dinner when Beak, who was a little boy about four years old, came to my house and said, "My papa wants to see you in his house." They were living in a little one-room shack about ten feet wide and sixteen feet long. His daughter, Fale, did their cooking under the trees outside. I walked over to his house. He saw me coming and pushed the door open from inside. He had a hat on his head and a serape wrapped around his shoulders. Very politely, almost too politely, he stepped aside and asked me to come into his home. I saw a fruit box on the extreme other end of the single room. I walked over to the box and sat down on it. Because he was acting so strangely, I was careful to rest my weight on the balls of my feet instead of on the box.

He took a key from under his serape and locked the door from the inside. Then, in broad daylight with me sitting on that box, he began to sneak up on me very slowly, with his right hand under the serape. Needless to say, I was tense, and watching him very closely. When he was about three feet from me, he pulled a dagger out from under the serape, raised it above his head, and made a dive for me. I came off the box about the same time he made his lunge. I caught his right arm in my left hand as he started down with the dagger and at the same time struck him on the jaw with all I had with my right hand. This knocked him down, semi-conscious. I picked up the dagger and walked back to my house. I told Dolly what had happened. She said, "What are you going to do?" I answered, "I don't know, but this is another one of those nights when we'll draw the curtains and have no lights on inside. I don't know what he might do."

The next morning I stepped out the door on my way to lay out the day's work for the hands. Paredes was standing there with Fale on one side and Beak on the other. All three were crying. I asked, "Paredes, what's the trouble?" He said, "Mi Patrón, you were lucky yesterday I did not kill you." He opened his shirt. His chest was covered with knife wounds. "Tengo miedo. Each time I get drunk, I will remember how you refused to loan me money and how I tried to kill you. I would try again, and sometime you would not be lucky. Because you are the best patrón I ever had, I want to be far away. When I get drunk on Saturday, I will sober up before I get to where you are."

The last I saw of them, the three were walking through the brush, headed south.

THE BENEFIT OF HIS JUDGMENT (1925)

I had a man drive into the yard one day. He told me he was handling a large block of real estate in the Valley, mostly land subject to irrigation, and he offered it to me at a rather attractive price with a small down payment. I went and looked at the land and told him I'd see if I could get the money together for the down payment. I'd let him know in the morning.

Because it was a large purchase and involved a lot of money, I went to my dad and told him I had a piece of land I wanted to show him. We looked at the land, and I asked him what he thought of it from the standpoint of quality and price. He wanted to know how many acres we were talking about. I told him around 1,500 acres. He said that would be more than $300,000. I said that was right. Then he asked me why I was showing him this land. I told him I was considering buying it and would like the benefit of his judgment. He rather quizzically asked if I would follow his judgment. We both laughed because I had always pretty much followed my own judgment rather than take advice from anyone. I said, "Possibly not, but it will help make up my mind." He said, "Well, if it was me, I wouldn't do it. If I owed more than a quarter of a million dollars, I wouldn't sleep another wink. But if I were you, I would do it because you won't worry a damn bit about it. I think you could put it over!" I said, "I think you've told me what I wanted to hear. I'm going to buy the property."

I did. It was the first large purchase of real estate I made.

WE'RE IN THE BANKING BUSINESS (1925)

Early in the 1920s, I had very little money. So when I found a deal I thought would work, I would go to various individuals who had money to loan and explain my deal. If they would furnish the money, I would handle the deal. They could keep a lien on the property until they got their money and the customary interest back; after that, we would split the deal fifty-fifty. Many people helped me, and I'm happy to say, not a single one ever lost any money in the ventures. The majority of the time they would double or triple their money in a matter of months. My problem was that I couldn't find investors fast enough.

As I was clearing this land, it became available for farming. Since I had cleared it for whoever owned it, I would have the first opportunity to rent it. This required money.

I went to the banker and explained the problem. He said, "Lloyd, you'll soon get more land than you can handle." I answered "No, these people clearing the land for me have experience farming on a small scale in Mexico. I can give these men as much land as they can handle." The workers usually determined this by how many children of working age (ten years old and up) were in the family. In Dakota on the farm we boys were told by Pop, "When you can walk, you can work."

I worked out a deal with some of the workers whereby I would buy a set of mules and the necessary machinery to handle the block of land I was turning over to them. Since all banks in that day and age were small and had about $5,000 to loan, I proposed to sell the mules and machinery to each farmer and take a mortgage against the mules and the machinery. The deal was, I would furnish grocery money through the year, money for seed, water, etc., and when the crop was harvested, I would sell it, deduct all the costs and split the profits fifty-fifty. This left them in a position that the bank could also have a mortgage on the crop.

I told the banker that what I wanted him to do was loan this money to these farmers whom I would supervise and manage, and I would personally endorse the notes. This way, each operation could borrow up to $5,000. The banker told me these would be hazardous notes, but if I was willing to pay what they were worth, he would handle a reasonable amount of the notes for me.

In this manner the amount of land I could handle was limited only to the amount of these notes that the bank would handle for me. If the money was available, it could run into a lot of money. Again, he told me that if I was willing to pay for it, he could handle quite a few of these notes.

The first man I took to the bank was a man by the name of Apolonio Ybarra, a man about sixty years old and not in very good health, but who had three young men and two young women staying at home. The banker said we ought to loan him $4,500 in order to stay under the $5,000 limit and that we would have a little more if we needed it. He also said this money would only be advanced as it was needed to do the farming, which meant we would probably borrow the money in September when the man moved onto the property. Then the money would be held by the bank and advanced in February, March, April, and May. Our harvest would be June, July, and August, so that the note would be paid in September.

The banker told Apolonio that he was taking a mortgage on the mules, machinery, and equipment that I had given him a bill of sale to, and also a mortgage on the crops he would be growing. Then when he drew the mortgage, he told my man to sign it. Apolonio replied, "No puedo leer ni escribir." The banker said, "All right, put your mark." Apolonio signed with an X. I endorsed the note.

The banker put the note in the bank and drew out $4,500 in cash. The first thing he did then was to take out $450 of the cash and put it in the bank as interest, in advance on the $4,500 loan for one year. Next, he drew from his desk drawer an application blank for life insurance and took an additional $120 for the insurance premium. So the money would be used an average of about three and a half months, but the $570 that he and the bank had for profit on earnings meant that we would have the use of $3930 for approximately three and a half months. When I got home, I figured that I was paying actually a little over 40 percent for the money I was using. But even that was less than the 50 percent I had been paying by splitting profits. But it was the only place I could get the money.

Now, back to the application for insurance. While Apolonio was sitting at his desk, the banker filled out the application that should have been filled out by a doctor. He took about fifteen years off Apolonio's age, took about thirty pounds off his weight, guessed his blood pressure to be what would satisfy the insurance company, and filled in the rest of the blanks originally completed by the doctor. I don't know what arrangement he had with the doctor who had to sign the applications or if he used somebody's name.

With this financing I began farming several thousand acres. I told the banker that I wasn't sure if a disaster was to strike, these loans would all be paid, but to the extent of my ability, they certainly would be. I also told him I didn't know how good the notes were, but that it should be profitable to the bank.

The statement he made to me was that the bank was broke anyway, but that the man that owned it was wealthy and could afford it. Every single one of these notes was paid.

In the 1929 crash this bank and almost every other bank were in trouble. Sometime in the early 1930s, the banker and the bank examiner came out to see me. They said the bank was in serious financial trouble. Unless new capital was supplied that day they were going to close their doors. The banker suggested that the bank had always been good to me. Now it was my job to help the bank. I told them, considering the interest I was paying the bank, I didn't really know how kind they had been to me.

Then they mentioned several widows who had all their life savings in the bank, as well as the old people who would lose all their money if the bank closed. Remember, this was before the days of Federal Deposit Insurance. I talked to my brother Elmer about it. We decided to replenish the capital, and we did. Within a week they were back, told me they had miscalculated and would need double the amount we had already contributed. That day I drove to Houston and the following morning talked to the First National Bank Examiner. They had several conversations with the owner of the bank and worked out a deal where the bank would remain open under the reorganization and would pay all the depositors. And we were in the banking business.

I met a young lawyer who had opened up a practice in Mission. He knew I had no education and no banking experience. He laughingly said to me, "Lloyd, what in hell do you know about the banking business?" I answered, "I don't know anything about the banking business, but if other people can do it, then so can I. I do know what is a good loan, and what isn't, and I guess that's one of the important functions of a bank." We had a young man in our office who had worked in his uncle's bank in Summerville, Texas. We started with him, and, like I said, we were in the banking business.

THAT'S A PRETTY BIG DRINK, BUT YOU CAN'T WASTE IT (about 1925)

We had just completed the building of a three-room office along the highway between Mission and McAllen. We had also poured a small vault where we could keep important papers. About the time we completed the pouring of the vault, a friend drove up in front of our new office and told us he had been over in Tennessee visiting his relatives. He had brought something back for us.

He went back to the trunk of his car, opened it, and lying in the trunk was a five-gallon keg of what he called Mountain Dew. He said it was a present for Elmer and me. We picked it up and carried it to our vault where it wouldn't be seen. This was during Prohibition. Of course, it had been illegally brought in from Tennessee.

He told us to have a drink on him out of this keg while the three of us could enjoy it together. We got a drill and drove a spigot into the keg. Our friend pulled out three small glasses. The moonshine was clear as water. Because it was prohibited, we all had to taste it. And while it looked innocent as water, one swallow was all you needed to know that as it went down your gullet, your tonsils were going to go along with it. It was liquid fire! We all coughed and decided we didn't need any more of it. So the keg lay there in our vault.

A few days later, a man walked into our office. He was about 6'6" and weighed probably 270 pounds. He stuck out a hand as big as a whole ham and introduced himself as Dick Wilson. We had heard a lot of stories about Mr. Wilson, and because they said he was probably the richest man in this part of Texas, we were glad to meet him. After visiting a few minutes, Mr. Wilson asked, "Do you have anything to drink in this office?" I started to say nothing but water, when I remembered the keg in the vault, and I said, "Yes." I turned to Elmer, "Why don't you get Mr. Wilson a drink out of the keg we have in the vault?"

Elmer emptied out the pitcher where we kept drinking water, went into the vault and came out holding the water pitcher half full of moonshine. The only glasses we had in the office were large water glasses. We set one in front of Mr. Wilson on the desk and Elmer started to pour, expecting him to say when to stop. He didn't. So Elmer proceeded to pour until this large water glass was full to the brim, with Mr. Wilson sitting there watching him. When the glass was full, Elmer set the pitcher down and said, "Help yourself."

Mr. Wilson took the glass in his huge hand, looked at it and said, "That's a pretty good size drink." He tipped it up. I knew when it hit his throat he would start coughing, but I was surprised. He drank it like he would drink water. When he had drunk half the glass, he stopped and said, "That's pretty good stuff, and that is a pretty big drink, but you can't waste it." He tipped it up and finished the drink! We visited a little more, and I expected to see him roll out of the chair, but he didn't. I couldn't see that the drink had affected him one bit.

Finally, after about an hour's visit, he said, "Well, I have to be going. Do you have any money in this office?" I said, "No, but I have a little money in my pocket." He asked, "How much?" and I answered "Five dollars." He said, "I would like to cash a check for five dollars because I am out, and I don't want to start out with my driver without at least a little money in my pocket." So he pulled out a little folding checkbook and asked me to make out a check to cash for five dollars. I did and handed him the checkbook for him to sign the check. He signed it, handed me the check, and I gave him the five dollars. Then he asked me to record the check in his checkbook and deduct it from the balance, showing what he still had in the bank in his personal checking account. It was the first time that I had experienced deducting five dollars from a bank balance of in excess of one million dollars. This was an impressive experience when I was having a very difficult time keeping my bank balance out of the red.

After this episode, I don't believe Mr. Wilson ever came to the Valley without stopping in our little office. We looked forward to interesting meetings and conversation each time he came by.

OKAY, YOU YELLOW BELLY, GO GET YOUR GUN (1929)

It was the 1929 crash. Banks were closing everywhere. Mr. Wilson owned the First National Bank of Mission. He had sold the stock in his bank to various purchasers, including us. We had bought $2,000 worth of the stock by our note in that amount, and I became a director in the bank. Times were very hard, and most of the banks that I was familiar with had a loan limit of $5,000. The first of these notes of one of the purchasers that came due was the note of the mayor of Mission. He told Mr. Wilson he could not pay the note, whereupon Mr. Wilson said he was going to pay it. This wound up in an argument, and Mr. Wilson filed suit to collect the note.

The next time Mr. Wilson was in the Valley, he was talking about the lawsuit on the note, which I was familiar with. I told him, "They're contending that the bank was broke at the time you sold the stock and that you knew it. My opinion is that with times as hard as they are and banks in as bad condition as they are, along with your reputation of being a very rich man, the jury will find against you on the sale of the note. I don't want you to misunderstand me, however, because we signed a note, and we're going to pay it." And we did. But to the best of my recollection, everyone else who owed the notes refused to make payment, at which time Mr. Wilson came to me and asked if we would be interested in buying the bank if he sold it entirely on time. I told him probably so, but if we did buy the bank he would have to agree to return the notes to the purchasers and let them return the stock that they had bought. I thought this was extremely important for the bank's good will in the community. Mr. Wilson refused to return the notes of the purchasers. So the matter went to court on the first note that was delinquent. The jurors' decision was as I had contemplated. The jury found that the bank was broke at the time the note was sold and that Mr. Wilson knew it.

The bank was about to close. In those days a stockholder in a bank could lose his stock and also was subject to a 100 percent assessment if the bank went broke. In addition to that, all deposits had been frozen in the bank, including a $100,000 deposit by Mr. Wilson, which he would lose if the bank closed. If, however, the bank remained open, once these deposits were unfrozen he could withdraw his $100,000. We discussed the matter. He was considering returning these notes, because after the first lawsuit results he had learned he could not collect them.

He came back to the Valley to talk to me about it, then went into the bank and talked to the cashier. The cashier told him that he had lost the lawsuit due to the prominence of the man he had sued and his many friends, but if it was handled right, with him representing Mr. Wilson, he could work out conditions on the notes to where he felt all the notes would be collected.

Mr. Wilson called me on the phone and asked me to come to the bank, which I did. He told me that he was willing to go ahead with the deal but he would not return the notes; he was going to collect them. I explained to him that it didn't make any difference to me—I had paid my note—except that I couldn't go through with the deal and have all this ill will against the bank. I told him that in reality he had implied that he would give these notes back, and that was the key to the deal we were trying to make. We got into a heated argument because I was already committed to many important depositors to get their note and return it to them in line with the agreement I thought we had with Mr. Wilson.

I think Mr. Wilson realized that he could not afford to press the issue too hard since we were the only prospect he had that would consider buying the bank. So as our argument cooled down a little, he said, "Take me down to The Manhattan Cafe and buy my lunch. We'll talk about it." I am sure he was thinking about the $100,000 deposit he had and the 100 percent assessment on the stock of which he owned at least 85 percent.

We sat down at a table in The Manhattan Cafe, but Mr. Wilson was still pretty mad at me for accusing him of crawfishing on his deal. I noticed as he picked up his coffee cup that his hand was shaking violently. Instead of trying to drink, he set the cup back down on the table. I looked across the room to a table close by, and there sat the mayor of Mission. Mr. Wilson turned to me, "There's the bastard that's responsible for all my troubles. If he ever speaks to me again, I will break this cane over his head." He had leaned a heavy cane against the table where we were sitting, eating our lunch. About the time he made the remark, the mayor and his friends had finished their meal, got up and walked by our table. The mayor said, "Hello, Lloyd," and I returned the greeting. Then he said, "Hello, Mr. Wilson." Remember, Mr. Wilson had just said, "If he ever speaks to me again, I will break this cane over his head," and he was certainly a man who intended to respect his word. So, with appropriate profanity, he grabbed that cane and struck for the mayor's head as hard as he could. Because he was sitting down and the mayor was standing up, the mayor was able to break the blow and prevent it from hitting him on the head. By that time, Mr. Wilson was on his feet, and so was I. I saw it could be a fight and immediately stepped between the two men while they were calling each other every name in the vocabulary of the frontier. Finally, Mr. Wilson said as I held them apart, "If I was twenty years younger, you S.O.B., I would drag you out of this building and stomp your guts out!" Whereupon the mayor replied, "If you were twenty years younger, you S.O.B., I would take you out on the street and beat the hell out of you." Then Mr. Wilson said, "Okay, you yellow belly, if you feel that way about it, go get your gun. We'll just settle it here, right in front of this cafe." I grabbed the mayor by the shoulder and shoved him through the door. I told him this had gone far enough. He didn't resist. Dick had gotten so mad at the mayor that he forgot all about his argument with me. He agreed to give the notes back, and he did.

The next morning I saw the mayor, and he remarked about the incident. I said, "Mr. Mayor, he did make you a proposition to go get your gun, and you would both settle it in front of the cafe. You didn't accept the challenge." The mayor said, "Well, Lloyd, the reason I didn't accept the challenge was because of the way his hand was shaking while we were arguing. I was thinking how in the hell do you dodge the bullets when a man's hand is shaking that much. He's bound to hit you with some of 'em." He could have been right.

REINFORCEMENTS WITH A SCREAM, A HOE, AND A BIG STICK (1926)

One day I came home and told Edna, "I'm going to straighten out this S.O.B. that stole some of my money." Edna said, "Lloyd, some of these fellows will kill you. What on earth will I do with two small children and a baby?" I said, "I've either got to leave the country or I've got to run my show. I won't have any trouble with him."

She said, "I'm going with you." She jumped in the car. Lloyd and Donny were little fellows. Lloyd was about six and Donny probably three. They jumped in too. We went out to the five-mile line where Juan Garcia lived. Earlier, one of his men had come up to me and said, "Do you know what Juan did with the money you gave him to chop the cotton?" I said, "No." He said, "He bought an automobile." I said, "He did?" He said, "Yes, it's on the side of the little house he lives in." We drove up to the back of the little house, and I stopped the car. Juan stepped out from the corner of the house. He was waiting for us and had seen us coming. He came up to the car. I said, "Juan, what did you do with that money I gave you to chop the cotton?" He said, "You guess," as sarcastic as the devil. I had promised Edna all the way out there that I wouldn't have any trouble with him but when he said, "You guess," that was too much. I leaped out of the car and went after Juan. And that's what he wanted— for me to chase him. I went around the corner of the house and when I did, there were three fellows with their backs up against the house. Two of them had axes and one had a grub hoe—all waiting for me. As I ran around the house I caught Juan by the shoulder and whirled him around. I figured I would just grab this guy and slam him up against the side of that car and hit as hard as I could before the other guys could get close enough to use the axes and grub hoe on me. As I shoved him up like that I pulled my hand back to hit him as hard as I could.

Then Edna screamed. If you ever heard Edna scream—she could get your attention. She had jumped out of the car and came around the corner of the house and let out that hideous yell. I didn't swing my hand all the way and I didn't hit this guy as hard as I intended to. I knew I'd better duck. I jumped to the side. One of these guys came down with the grub hoe, and it went deep into the ground. I had let Juan go. He said, "I'll get the gun." I knew the gun would be in the house. I ran around the house where the door was and got there before Juan did. When he got there I was standing in the door. Edna was out there jumping up and down screaming hysterically. This was before Kenneth was born. But I was occupied. Three guys were closing in on me. I was still standing by the door. I made a dive for one of these guys like I was going to grab him. He struck with the ax. When he struck I jumped back and grabbed the ax, just jerked it out of his hand. Out into the cotton field he went.

When I looked up, here came the boys running around the corner of the house. Lloyd had picked up a hoe. He had decided he was going to get into this fracas. Donny had picked up a big stick, which he had over his shoulder.

The men ran into the cotton field. We took Juan's car away from him and fired him.

BACK YOUR JUDGMENT (1926)

Among the many interesting people I have met in my lifetime, I recall one very unusual person. His name was Joe Abraham. He was a Syrian of Jewish faith, unusual in that he was an immigrant to this country from Syria and that he had never gone to school a day in his life. He started out from New York City, working west, selling pencils and pencil sharpeners, and finally landed in Bristow, Oklahoma. He first got a job in a store. After a short while the storekeeper wanted to retire and sold Joe the store entirely on time. He began operating the store and, when he could do so, allowed people to buy groceries on credit. When they could not get the cash to pay their bills, they would give him a piece of real estate or a portion of the minerals under the real estate. When I first knew Joe Abraham, he was very proud of the fact that he had ten million dollars in government bonds, and well he might be. At that time ten million dollars was quite a sizable fortune, and strangely enough, Mr. Abraham still signed his name with an X.

For some reason he took a liking to me, and when I was driving around the country a lot, he would come and ride with me, and we would talk. He was always telling me about good deals he had made that worked out exceedingly well financially. I asked him one time, "If it's so easy to make a fortune, would you tell a young fellow like me some of your secrets?" He thought a minute, then said that there was no secret or magic to making a success. The real key to success was three little words. I asked him to tell me those three little words. He laughed and with a heavy accent answered, "The three words are the plainest kind of common sense. They are: Back Your Judgment." I laughed and asked, "Suppose your judgment isn't any good?" He smiled, "Make a few mistakes—pretty soon you're pretty smart." Then he elaborated. "The smartest men in the world are not necessarily the richest, and the richest men in the world are not necessarily the smartest. The rich men generally are the men with guts; in other words, they had the nerve to back their judgment." He elaborated further to prove the point. "If you were the smartest man in the world, and knew everything that was going to transpire and when, but still lacked the nerve to back your judgment and do something about it, you would never have any money." So his advice was to study every proposition you came across to see what the possibilities of failure and possibilities of success were. If the possibilities of success were many times greater than the possibilities of failure, then back your judgment, and do something about it. Joe concluded, "Lloyd, always limit your exposure as much as possible but, nevertheless, do something about it rather than wish you had later. Most of the people I have met tell me, 'I could have done so-and-so, but lacked the nerve to take the chance.'"

CANALS GET CONCRETED AND FEUDS GET SETTLED (1926)

In the early development in the Rio Grande Valley, the irrigation canals were built by using mules and scrapers. The soil, being largely alluvial silt, was quite porous, and in a few years the seepage from these canals began to destroy the lands adjacent to the canals. The people soon realized that the canals would have to be lined to preserve the land.

To begin with, the developer would buy a large tract of land to make the canals. He would begin selling land, explaining to the prospective purchasers that the land was subject to irrigation through these canals and that, of course, the water was being pumped from the river.

Shortly after a lot of land had been sold, a protracted drought developed over South Texas. There was no water in the river. The people who had invested, in many cases their life savings, in the land and the crops they had planted faced disaster because of the drought and the lack of water. Bitter feelings developed between many of the purchasers and the developer of the land. Hundreds of lawsuits were filed. At about the same time, the political situation became very bad and, in many cases, intense, due to political corruption. The Good Government League was formed. It challenged the autocratic authority of political machines long in control. It was almost a case of choosing up sides. Bitter fights, turmoil, murders, assassinations—the Valley became almost an armed camp.

New families were moving in continually, among them a family by the name of Gordon, including a son-in-law by the name of Mullins. This Mullins had been working in Oklahoma on air hammers and the like and had developed a beautiful set of muscles that he liked to show off. He liked to work without a shirt because his muscles showed up exceptionally well. He had hired a few laborers, and they finally got to where they wouldn't work for him because at almost any excuse he would beat them up just because he apparently enjoyed doing so. Mullins immediately joined a number of people who had filed lawsuits against the developer, and in the face of this continuing battle, the developer realized that the people who had the land would have to line the irrigation canals. The only manner in which this could be done was by a bond issue, which would be a lien on the lands that these people had bought. There was no alternative. However, feelings had become so intense that the landowners were divided about evenly. Those who would support the concrete canal program and those who took the attitude that because the developer wanted it they wanted to oppose it and probably have the personal satisfaction of breaking him. They felt they had already lost everything.

An election was held. The opposition to the program was successful in defeating the issue. The developer called me to his home and told me that if the program was not successful, many of the people would lose their lands through seepage, and ultimately what would otherwise be a Garden of Eden would be a salty, barren wasteland. I told him that in my opinion the issue of concrete canals had to be separated from his quarrel with the people who had filed their lawsuits for damages because the river had gone dry. Therefore, I figured the program was defeated because it was his organization leading the fight for concrete canals. I felt if they would schedule another vote as soon as sufficient time had elapsed, that we could have one meeting at the Wimodasis Clubhouse and also one at the Sharyland School on two nights prior to the second election. I was sure that if the developer stayed out of the fight we could probably get enough support to carry the election. He said he doubted it, but the matter was so urgent that another try had to be made. He asked me if I would undertake the job. I told him I would because I also had bought a lot of land that would become worthless without the protection of the concrete canals.

When sufficient time had elapsed, a second election was called. We had the meetings as scheduled prior to the date of the election. At the meeting at the Wimodasis Clubhouse, I got up to explain the program at seven in the evening and was still on the floor when the meeting broke up. First, there was a lot of angry shouting by the opposition, but little by little I was able to build up support. More and more people realized that this was not a fight between some of the people and the developer, but purely a question of concrete canals. The meeting at the Sharyland School was the following night. The man Mullins had heard that I had called the meetings on the concrete canals and had finally gotten the Wimodasis crowd settled down to consider the issue on its merits. He vowed that he would break up the meeting at the Sharyland School. The meeting was chaired by an elderly gentleman by the name of Charley Rhea. He had gotten up to ask me to take the floor and explain the issue to the gathering. There were probably three hundred people there. When I got up, the opposition had been very well organized and had made up their minds that the people were not going to hear what I had to say, but little by little I got them to understand we were talking about their future and the future of their children. This was not for anything but the protection of their land. It was what we had to do or move out.

Mr. Mullins saw that we were making headway, so he decided the time had come for action. He got up from his seat in the back of the room and slowly walked up to the front. He made the remark to Mr. Rhea, who attempted to block his passage, that I needed to be thrown off the platform. Mr. Rhea stepped in front of him, and I realized that he was no match for Mullins, so I stepped over on the platform where Mr. Rhea was trying to block Mullins and said, "Mr. Rhea, if Mr. Mullins wants up on the stage, it is perfectly all right with me, and if he wants to attempt to throw me off this stage, the crowd will have a better show than they intended to have when they came here." I think Mr. Mullins had been in the habit of frightening a lot of people, and I suddenly realized there was some indecision as to whether he wanted to attempt what he had in mind. I didn't confront him. I simply stepped back on the stage, ignoring him completely, and proceeded to explain the purpose of the meeting, and the need. He stood at the edge of the platform for two or three minutes. Some of the people who were probably for the concrete canals shouted to him two or three times to ask him why he was hesitating and why he didn't get up on the stage. He finally whirled around and left the meeting. The following Saturday the election was held. The issue carried.

The following Monday morning I was sitting at my desk in my office when Mullins walked in. He was almost hysterical when he rushed up to my desk and shouted, "You won the election, but the fight is not over. I'm going to fight you until I spend every dollar I own. I will sell my cattle, my chickens, my turkeys, my home, and fight you. If I don't win, I will kill you." I reached in the drawer of my desk where I had a .45 pistol. I pulled the drawer open. When he saw I had a gun, he was shocked and a little pale because I think he thought I was going to use it, but I slid it across the top of my desk to him, and said, "Here, Ernest, is a better gun than you will ever own, and it's loaded. Why don't you take it and start shooting?" He looked at the pistol sliding across the top of my desk, jumped to his feet, and shouted, "You're crazy and a damn fool," and ran out of my office.

About a month after that date, he came to a little office I had in my home where I paid my laborers each Saturday. It was a large room and fifteen or twenty of my men were in the room standing up waiting for their checks, while I was sitting at the desk figuring their time and signing their checks. He walked back and forth in the room and did not speak to me. I presumed he came to pick a quarrel, but I was going to let him carry the ball. After walking back and forth a half dozen times, he noticed some well-worn boxing gloves hanging on the wall at one end of my room. When he saw them, he said, "That's what I've been looking for." He went over and took down one pair of the gloves and said to one of my men, "Tie these on me." The man did as he was told.

Then Mullins strutted back and forth behind my chair. After a while, as he walked behind me, he hit me lightly on the back of my head. I didn't say a word, but kept on working, and he walked back and forth three or four times and then hit me another light blow on the head. When I didn't say anything, he finally said, "Do I have to knock you off that chair to get you to put on that other pair of gloves?" I replied, "No, Ernest. If a man hit me in the back of the head one time, I would consider it an accident. If he did it again, I might think it was an accident, but probably not. If he ever did it the third time, I would know it wasn't an accident. Then I would put on the other pair of gloves." He said, "So that's the way it is, is it?" and I said, "That's the way it is." Whereupon, he hit me a pretty solid blow on the back of the head. I got up and told the same fellow to tie the other pair of gloves on my hands.

At that time, Mullins probably did not give any thought to the possibility that I was the person that had practically worn out that pair of boxing gloves. Anyway, I squared off, thinking he would do so and then we would test each other out. He did not. As soon as I squared off, he backed up about eight feet, raised his hands, and actually ran toward me. When he was about ready to make contact, he swung his right hand in a circle over his head and came down with his fist like he was going to drive a post in the ground. It was easy to throw up my left forearm and block the blow, and I was amazed because he showed no semblance of boxing. He backed up to the wall and repeated the same performance. Again I blocked him and was astonished that he apparently knew so little about boxing because practically all the people I knew were generally pretty good boxers. The third time he came at me, he started in the same manner as he had twice before; and I feigned a little with my left, but drove a solid right cross to the side of his head. The fact that he was coming in rapidly at the same time I stepped forward and delivered the right cross made the blow even a little harder than I intended. He flew backward and, if it had not been for the proximity of the wall, would have gone down. His back and head hit the wall a very solid blow. He opened his mouth and blood was running out of his mouth. He stepped away from the wall as if he would try again, but he changed his mind, slammed his back to the wall, turned to the Mexican boy, and said, "Take these damned things off before somebody gets hurt." He then strode from the room without saying another word.

For the next couple of years, we would run into each other from time to time. I would speak, but he would not. My business had grown and I had brought a young lawyer into my office. One day he came in to me and said "Did you see where the Irrigation District is foreclosing Mullins's home under flat rate?" I said, "No, I hadn't," and asked how much the suit was for. He said it was $2,800. The reason he mentioned it being for flat rate was because we both knew that if property was sold for taxes, the owner then has a two-year period for redemption, but not so on flat rate. If sold under flat rate the sale is final with no redemption. I told my lawyer, "I am sure that Mullins will protect his property." Then he said, "I doubt it. I doubt if he can after building that new home. He has stretched his credit to the limit and has a lot of unpaid bills." I said, "Judge, you go to the sale and you bid judgment and costs." He said, "If you get the property, who takes title?" I replied, "Well, I don't think that will happen, but if it does, take the title in me." Strangely enough, that is what happened, and I am sure that Ernest thought that I had done this for revenge. Judge Dohrn filed the deed of record, and I said nothing to Mullins about it. Neither did the judge. Mullins continued to live in the house for the next two and a half years, taking all the income from the property with me paying the taxes and insurance on the house.

About two and a half years later, I drove by the place and saw about fifteen acres of spinach. Spinach was selling at a very high price, so the crop would be quite profitable. I asked the people who were harvesting this spinach where they were selling it, and they said they were selling it to the Bohannan Cannery. I drove in and talked to Mr. Bohannan, and asked him how much spinach had been delivered, and he told me something over $4,000 worth. I told him that I wanted him to give me a check for $1,500 and I would apply it on what Mullins owed me. He said he couldn't do that, and I told him I would stand between him and any trouble, and that if he would not do it I would have to go and get a lawyer and tie up the entire crop because I had title to the property. So he gave me the check. The original amount had increased considerably, with taxes, insurance, et cetera, so I applied this $1,500 check to the overall total I had in the property.

About a year later, Mullins met my attorney, and he said, "What in the hell is Lloyd going to do with that property?" My attorney said, "He doesn't intend to do anything with it." Mullins said, "But he owns it." My lawyer said, "He doesn't look at it like that. He just wants you to pay him what you owe him." The property had increased tremendously in value, and he said to the lawyer, "Are you telling me that if I paid him what he had in the property and interest and other expenses, he would let me have my home?" My attorney said, "That is what he told me he had in mind." Mullins said, "I can't believe it, and I don't," and walked out of the office. About a month later, he came by and asked the lawyer what the balance I considered I had coming amounted to. My lawyer figured it up and said it looked like $3,200. Mullins said, "Are you telling me that if I paid that amount, Lloyd would give me a deed to the property?" The judge said, "I think so. Why don't you find out?" He went to the bank in Mission, bought a cashier's check, and came out and handed it to Judge Dohrn, and said, "I am giving you the money, but I don't believe it. That property is worth ten to twelve times what he has against it." Judge Dohrn reached in the drawer of his desk and pulled out a warranty deed that was already executed in Mullins's favor. It was a cash deed. Dohrn said, "Ernest, Lloyd executed this a year ago and it has been lying in my desk. He wanted this executed so that if anything happened to him, you would not lose your home." Ernest said, "I have always thought he was a damn fool; now I know he is," and then asked Judge Dohrn to file the deed of record for him.

About ninety days later, he came into my office and said, "I think it's about time I came to tell you that I agree with my wife. She says you are a hell of a fine fellow." We became very good friends, and many times talked about his first boxing lesson.

IT WASN'T RIPE! (1928)

In the early days, money was scarce. It was important to have a garden where we could raise much of the food used in the home. We raised potatoes, beans, peas, cabbage, cucumbers, tomatoes, cantaloupe, and watermelons—all the usual things found in a Southern garden.

The thing that created the greatest interest among the children was, of course, the watermelons. Someone had told Lloyd Jr. and Don that if they placed a vessel of water close to the feelers of the watermelon that the feelers would draw the water to the vine and grow larger melons. The boys had done this on several of the vines, and it seemed to be having great results. Their melons were growing unusually large. They had also been told that if they would protect these big melons from the sun they would not sunburn and therefore be even better melons. So each day they pulled fresh weeds and grass and laid them over the melons.

Lloyd was about seven at the time and Don, probably four. The boys played together all the time, so when Lloyd started school in Sharyland, Don was lonesome. And because he had more time on his hands since Lloyd was going to school, Don wondered, day after day, when the first watermelon would be ripe and ready to eat. Each day he suggested to Lloyd that they plug it and find out whether it was ripe or not. Each day Lloyd consistently told him, "We are going to wait 'til Dad tells us it's good and ripe."

This particular day I noticed Don at the corner of the yard about three in the afternoon, and I knew he was lonesome and waiting for Lloyd to come home from school. Each afternoon when Lloyd returned he and Don would run to the garden, uncover the melons, look at them, and speculate when they would be ripe—and especially when they could start eating them. But this day was different. Don saw Lloyd coming, walking across the tracks. He came over to where Don was standing, and they started walking toward the garden and the watermelons. I heard the conversation, and it went like this: "Hello, Benny." "Hello, Don." As they walked along toward the watermelons, Don said, "Benny, you know that watermelon of ours?" Lloyd turned to Don and answered suspiciously, "Yes." "Well," Don said, and hesitated a little. With Lloyd watching him closely, he spoke again, "Well, it wasn't ripe!"

Lloyd yelled, "Don, did you plug that watermelon?" They both ran for the watermelons. I knew there would be trouble. Lloyd jerked the cover off the watermelon and there was a big plug cut about four inches square, and, as Don had said, it wasn't ripe.

I knew the only way to restore the peace was to take both boys to town and buy them the biggest Black Diamond watermelon I could find, already cold and ready to slice.

Thereafter, Don waited until the three of us decided each melon was ripe and ready to eat.

THREE-DOLLAR LAND (1930)

One of the early large tracts of land that we bought was purchased from the original "Wildcatter," Tom Slick.

A stranger walked up to me, introduced himself as Tom Slick, and told me that he had a tract of land that he wanted to sell me. I told him I was sorry, but I didn't have any money. He laughed and said, "You don't need any money." I said, "Then I am interested." He said, "Let me show you the land." We drove out into the McCook district, which was all brush at that time with trails running through the brush. He told me that this was the beginning of the property. After riding several miles through the brush, I said, "Mr. Slick, just how much land are you showing me?" He said, "It will run into many thousands of acres—I don't know the exact acreage. I want to tell you exactly what I am doing. I have bought this land for $7 an acre, cash, which includes all the materials. What I am proposing to you is that I sell it to you on a nothing-down basis, retaining all the minerals myself, with twenty years to pay, at 5 percent. In this manner, when you have paid for the land, I will own the minerals for nothing." I said, "Well, it is really the surface I am interested in, and on this kind of basis, I think we can handle it." So, I bought our first large tract of land, and for $7 an acre.

Word got around very rapidly, and a couple of days later, as I was driving down the main street of Mission, two old-timers, both of them large ranchers, were standing on the sidewalk when they hailed me. There were no paved streets, and I made a U-turn and pulled up to the curb, got out, and shook hands with both of them. One of them said, "Is it true that you bought the Slick land for $7 an acre?" I said, "Yes, it's true." He put his hand up to his mouth as if to tell me a secret, and said, very sarcastically, "Is there gold under that land?" I said, "No, and there doesn't need to be. I am a firm believer that every foot of that land will some day be worth $150 an acre. When I was a small boy, my father and mother homesteaded in South Dakota at a time when they could buy all the land they wanted in the Indian Territory for a few cents an acre, and Dakota was Indian Territory at that time. When I went into the service in 1917, that land they could have bought for a few cents an acre was worth $160 an acre. This area of the country has a longer growing season, and the soil I have been looking at out there will grow better and more profitable crops than the land I am referring to in South Dakota. I am a firm believer that every section of the United States will grow and increase in value until it duplicates the value of the already developed sections of the country that have the same natural advantages. This is not only what will happen here, but is what has happened as the population moves from the East to the West. So, what I am saying is that this is what is happening, and is history where the country has already been developed, and has to happen here."

He said, "You are crazy! That is $3 land, and will never be worth a dime more." My reply was, "I agree that one of us may be crazy, but I am inclined to believe that time will prove you wrong."

Years later, as this land was in cultivation and producing, I would see my friends at times in Mission and McAllen, and I would say, "Let me take you out and show you the $3 land." Their good-natured reply was, "Oh, you go to hell!"

DAYS OF AL CAPONE (1931)

It was the Depression and money was tight. I had to head north to collect on notes owed us, or we couldn't stay in business. Betty had just been born and Kenneth was five years old. So I took Lloyd and Don along on the trip. They were fine company. At the beginning of the trip we stopped in San Antonio to visit Mom and Pop. They fed us well. Then Mom cut a little pillow in half, stitched up the open sides, and gave each boy his own pillow. She knew we would be driving day and night. I drove like I breathed. We sang songs like "Jim O'Shea was cast away upon a native isle. The natives there they liked his hair, they liked his Irish smile." If we didn't know all the words, we made them up. Roadside fruit stands along the way furnished most of our meals.

Collecting notes along the way, we finally got to Chicago. It was 2:30 in the morning and the Stevens Hotel had finished serving food for the night. We headed out on State Street for a bite for the boys before going to bed. We found a café and ordered bacon and eggs. While we were waiting for our order a hophead leaped through the swinging doors screaming for help! He ran toward the back door where two thugs were staked, covering him with sawed off shotguns and a tommy gun. He whirled to face the front door when five more men, heavily armed, shoved through. There was only one girl in attendance. One of the men told her to stand where she was and let the food burn. He grabbed the telephone, jerked it off the wall, and threw it on the floor so help could not be called. He told us to sit where we were and began to tell the hophead what they were going to do to him and how they were going to do it for his having a part in torturing and killing some of the Capone gang. The hophead was going to be the lesson that would make others shudder when they thought of anything like that. I saw he was going crazy—if not already there. The situation could only deteriorate.

So I told the boys there wasn't any food for us, and I was sure the gangsters didn't want witnesses. So we'd better try to leave. I wanted them to do exactly as I told them. I told them I was going to stand up. As I did Lloyd would crowd right behind me and Don right behind him. Stop for nothing. As we stepped through the door I told them not to run but to step in front of me and walk as fast as they could for the car, then open the door and jump in. I said, "Now!" We all stood up, and they told us to sit down. We didn't hesitate, but walked directly for the door. They covered us with their guns and cursed us. We never slowed. They were shoulder to shoulder. I said, "Gangway, comin' through." Dropping my shoulders low, I gave the first a mighty heave and each nearly knocked the next man over so the whole line nearly went down, taken entirely by surprise.

The boys were in front of me. I couldn't keep up with their walk. They were in the car in a flash. Behind me the air was blue with cursing and ordering me back. I could almost feel the bullets tickling my spine, but none were fired. I got in the car, headed down State Street, and asked the boys if they were hungry. They said, "No!"

The next morning in the paper we read that there had been a gangster killing on State Street.

Incidentally, I later realized that a very nice Stetson I had bought the week before must have been left in that café.

Lloyd Bentsen Sr., c. 1940.

Lloyd Jr. and Don, c. 1927.

Dolly Bentsen and Kenneth, c. 1927.

Betty Ellen Bentsen advertising Rio Grande Valley grapefruit, c. 1934.

Dolly Bentsen with Kenneth and Betty, c. 1935.

Lloyd and Dolly Bentsen and their children, Lloyd Jr., Don, Kenneth, and Betty, c. 1934.

The Bentsen family during World War II. Left to right, Kenneth, Lloyd Sr., Betty, Edna Ruth "Dolly," Lloyd Jr., and Donald.

Left: Dolly Bentsen and Lloyd Jr. 1971.

Below: Dolly Bentsen, seated, with Lloyd Bentsen Sr., left, Lloyd Bentsen Jr., Lyndon B. Johnson, and John Connally, c. 1971.

Lloyd Bentsen Sr. receiving an award from the Texas State Guard, 1963.

Lloyd Bentsen Jr., Lloyd Bentsen Sr., and Don Bentsen on a hunting trip on the Rincón Ranch, c. 1983.

Lloyd Bentsen Sr. and Lloyd Bentsen Jr. on a fishing trip in Alaska, c. 1980.

Lloyd Bentsen Sr. and family members at a historical marker dedication at Bentsen State Park, Mission, 1986. From left, David and Susan Winn Lowry, Lloyd Bentsen Sr., Betty and Dan Winn, and Dan Winn Jr.

Lloyd Bentsen Sr. with his children, grandchildren, and great-grandchildren, 1985.
Photo by Gittings.

Patriarch

1 – AND THESE DUCKS – HAD THE WRONG DATE (1945)

We had acquired a number of ranches around the town of Clarksville, Texas. Among them was a ranch called Kymish. It joined the Red River across from Oklahoma. Adjacent to the river were several small freshwater lakes. They were ideal for duck and goose hunting in the early fall when the ducks and geese were migrating.

One morning our attorney, Judge Edwards, called and told me that the hunting season was opening the following morning. If I would come, he would meet me at the Kymish Ranch, where greenhead mallards were coming in by the thousands. I told him I would be there. I drove all night. The next morning when the sun came up, I was on the Kymish Ranch.

I went down to one of these little lakes and decided that as thick as the ducks were, I would limit my shooting to the greenhead drakes, not shooting any hens. I was doing great, and the ground was covered with greenhead mallards when I saw a car coming toward the lake. As the car came closer, I realized it was Judge Edwards coming to join me. I walked over to his car. He was excited. "Lloyd, I made a mistake." I asked, "What's the mistake?" He said, "Well, duck season doesn't open until next week. You're a week early." I replied, "Well, I— and these ducks—had the wrong date. What do we do with the ducks?"

Judge Edwards chuckled, "Put them in the trunk of my car. I'll take them home and eat them, and you won't have to go to jail. Every time we have roast duck, we will think of you."

"SOME SHOT!" (1946)

The war was over. Our three sons were home from the service—strong, remarkable men. While we had great hunting and trapping in South Dakota and Northern Minnesota, we had all read and heard about bear and moose and caribou hunting in the Far North. I arranged a trip into northern Canada. We were to hunt on the line between Yukon, Canada, and Yukon, Alaska.

We left Dolly, Betty, B. A., Lloyd III, and the nursemaid at Lake Louise—all well cared for—as we set out on our hunt. We sent our Twin Beech and pilot home from Calgary. Lloyd Jr., Don, Kenneth, and I were carried by bus about eighty miles north of White Horse along the Alcan Highway that runs from White Horse to Dawson. After getting off the bus, we got on horseback. With several guides we rode back into the mountains, some fifteen hours of steady riding. The guides went ahead and set up camp on the banks of the river. The cook was waiting for us with hot, delicious caribou steaks as we climbed off our horses. The hour was quite late, but the twilight held on that season of the year until about 10:30 in the evening. The scenery was fantastically beautiful.

The river was extremely swift and the waters quite deep. Our guides told us we would cross the river in the morning and hunt to the south and west of the camp, each of us with his own guide. I had ridden many horses in my lifetime that were great at swimming rivers, but I had doubts whether the horses we had could swim this river when I saw this rushing water. I expressed my opinion. The guides explained that in the morning the water would only be inches deep. Most mornings it might even be frozen over. What was happening was each day in clear weather the sun would shine on the snowcapped mountains and the glaciers. The water would begin trickling down the sides of the mountain and would reach the streams generally about noon. The water would rapidly build up to where by six in the afternoon the stream would be a full-blown river. By midnight it would be a torrent. The cycle would continue as the sun lost its heat in the late afternoon, the thawing stopped, and the river would again be a tiny stream by morning.

We hunted on horseback. Each of us rode with his own guide, also on horseback, and two packhorses to carry guns, ammunition, and supplies of various kinds. They would also carry trophies back to camp.

We were 100 to 150 miles from the nearest settlement. The area was so vast it was breathtaking. We could take a telescope and spot the game on the mountains. We could see bear, caribou, moose, and mountain sheep halfway up the mountain. Most of the hunting was done at an elevation of 7,000 to 12,000 feet. Our horses were mountain-bred. As we climbed, they followed the various game trails in the general direction they normally traveled. The game trails generally went through very rugged parts of the mountains. A trail would often be on the steep side of the mountain where, if you lost your balance or your horse lost its footing, you might slide or roll hundreds of feet. On the other side you could reach out your hand many times and touch the side of the mountain.

We all carried tin cups with us. When you were thirsty, you could stop your horse at little streams trickling down the side of the mountain, fill your cup and drink the most delicious water you ever tasted because there was no smoke or contamination of any kind. We would say that water was just like the Lord originally intended water to be. Weeks after we left the mountains, we wished for another drink of that delicious water.

Sometimes the horses could climb all the way up the mountain. But most of the time it became so steep that you had to dismount and climb several hundred feet by inching up the side of the mountain, pulling yourself up by twigs and branches and finding footholds in the rocks. When you reached these peaks, you would stop, take out your telescope, and search the neighboring mountains and peaks for the game you were wanting.

Many strange things happened to each of us on the trips we made daily. Everyone knew there would be nights when certain of the hunters would not come in that night. They could get a big bear late in the afternoon, and by the time he was skinned out and packed, it was too late to cross the river and streams because of the high water. You would get out your sleeping bags and grub and camp out. We all experienced this. It added a great deal of pleasure to our hunting trip.

One day my guide, who was called Moose, a tall, slender Indian and certainly the best guide I have ever known, told me that this day we would hunt sheep. This was the number one trophy of the area. Usually they ranged early in the fall from 10,000 to 12,000 feet elevation. He told me he knew an area where he had seen some good heads.

We were able to ride our horses to about 11,500 feet elevation. Then it grew so steep that we had to climb the rest of the way on foot.

I was in excellent physical condition, and walking was never a problem. But as we dismounted from our horses, Moose turned to me, pointed to the peak, and said, "There's where we're going. You go on. I'll feed the horses and picket them, then go up and make tea and lunch. We'll eat when you get there." The peak we were looking at was quite steep, but not over five hundred feet. I turned to him and said, "What did you say?" He repeated what he had said. I laughed, "You can do what you like, but I will be up there with you—watching you prepare that tea and lunch." He laughed, because he knew something I didn't know.

I started to walk and had not gone fifty feet until I was completely out of breath and my legs seemed to have lost their strength. The best I could do was take three or four steps, then stop and rest. A little later, Moose walked by on his way to the peak. When I finally made it, the tea and lunch were ready. We sat down and enjoyed it. Moose had been living in the high country, but this was a completely new experience for me. After we had finished our lunch, we walked along the ridge for probably a quarter of a mile. So long as we were not climbing, it didn't bother me that much.

We finally came to a little plateau that was a ridge on the top of the range of mountains. It looked quite rugged, but almost level for what seemed to be a mile or a mile and a half. It was an unusual rock formation. Moose suddenly became excited and stepped off this ridge and among some rocks. He told me to follow, which I did. Then he took out his telescope and looked down along the ridge to where he saw a blotch of white lying in the snow. He handed the telescope to me and said, "Look." I put the scope to my eye. The blotch of white was a tremendous Dall ram with the most magnificent horns I had ever seen. Moose tapped me on the shoulder and said, "There's your trophy." I asked, "How do I get to him?" He said, "You stay under cover. Me, too. When he gets tired of resting, he'll walk away farther or come toward us. Maybe you'll get a shot."

From our cover we watched this marvelous ram for at least five hours.

He was just lying in the sunshine, chewing his cud. He never got up. Finally Moose said, "If we're going to get across the river and get back to camp, we have to go now. Later the river will be too deep to cross and since there are so many bear here we don't want to sleep out tonight." This was such a gorgeous trophy that I decided to have one more look before I left him. Moose and I both intended to come back the next day and see if we could get another chance at this ram. But, since I wanted to take one more look and since I had a good 10-power scope on my rifle, I laid the rifle across a rock to take a rest while I was studying the ram.

Moose thought I was going to fire, which I had no intention of doing because of the extreme distance. He said, "You have a rifle that shoots that far? Try and drop a bullet past him. Maybe he'll run this way and you'll get a shot." The thought came to my mind that instead of trying to drop a bullet past him—since I was shooting in that direction anyway—why not try to hit him? At least I might be able to get the bullet close to the ram. I made up my mind to fire the shell. Having plenty of time, I took off my hunting jacket and laid it across two rocks that formed a wedge. Then I pressed my rifle down in the wedge until it was very solid. Lying down to look through the scope, I tapped the butt of my rifle until I thought the LEA dot in my scope was probably nine and a half feet above the ram's shoulder. My scope was equipped with a half-inch LEA dot, rather than the seven-inch, and also a very tiny vertical crosshair. The crosshair crossed the center of his shoulder. Then I took another rock and set it up against the butt of my rifle, taking my hunting cap and wedging it between the rock and the butt of the gun to absorb some of the recoil. I checked the scope again. It had not moved.

At this elevation there was no cross wind, simply a dead calm, and I didn't have any question of drifting. I didn't touch the gun, but put my thumb on the trigger guard and my finger on the trigger and gently squeezed it off. The recoil of the gun ripped it out of the wedge I had shoved it into. To avoid having the gun fall and probably hit my scope on the rocks, I grabbed for the gun and caught it. And therefore I did not see where my bullet had gone. Moose hollered, "Some shot!" With my gun retrieved, I looked toward the ram. He was rolling off the peak where he had been lying and stopped about six feet from there. Moose and I stepped off the distance down the ridge. Our nearest calculation was that my bullet had traveled over 900 yards. The bullet had gone through the center of the ram's shoulder. Moose told me that never in his life had he hunted with a hunter who could compare to me with a rifle. I was glad to let him think I was that kind of hunter, although I was just as surprised as the ram and Moose were. It did have one side effect—Moose believed I could shoot anything I could see. Thereafter, when we saw game, Moose didn't want me to maneuver for position. He simply wanted me to shoot it wherever it was, but now I had a reputation to protect. So I stubbornly, against his wishes, maneuvered for position while he was saying, "Shoot! You'll kill him from here!" The rifle I was shooting was a 300 H&H Magnum with a 150-grain bullet. I had adjusted the rifle in at 450 yards because I had expected, in that country, to have to make some long shots.

By the time we had skinned out the ram, prepared the trophy, and got it packed, it was way too late to cross the river. So we made camp where our horses had been picketed, prepared our bedrolls, and decided to get some sleep. It was cold at that high elevation and at that time of year. So we zipped our sleeping bags up over our heads. About one in the morning, I heard a lot of commotion from the direction of our horses. Of course, the first thing you suspect is a grizzly. Without taking my head out of the sleeping bag, I said, "Moose, something is bothering our horses." All I heard was a very terse "Shut up!" Needless to say, I was furious, but the horses seemed to have quieted down. I made up my mind that in the morning my guide and I would reach an understanding about how we talked to one another, or I would fire him. I dropped off to sleep. The next morning when I woke up, still furious, I zipped open my sleeping bag. Moose was standing in front of it. He asked, "Did you see what happened last night?" He showed me a grizzly's track. The huge grizzly had walked between his and my sleeping bags, which were not more than eight feet apart. He said, "You move or talk last night, he knocks your head off."

I did not discuss the incident further, but I now understood the terseness of his remark the night before!

BY WESTERN UNION ... (1947)

I spent one anniversary away from Dolly all the time we were married. This is how it happened. It was two days before our wedding anniversary. I said, "Dolly, I've got to go to Des Moines, Iowa, on a deal." (In those days there weren't planes flying back and forth.) She said, "You won't be home for our anniversary?" I said, "Oh, Dolly, yes I will. I can drive all night tonight, be there tomorrow sometime, close my deal, and drive all night the next night. I'll be back here for our anniversary." She said, "I don't like you driving all those nights in a row." "Doesn't bother me. I'm used to it," I laughed. "All right," she said.

When I got to Des Moines, the snow was coming down in torrents. I guess it snowed all night long. The roads were all closed and the trains were all stopped. Passages were full of snow and they hadn't gotten the snowplows out. Dolly was sitting in Texas not knowing I was snowbound in Iowa. I tried to phone, but there was no way I could get word to her. Maybe a telegram? They told me I might get through if the lines were open in the morning. So I started with the idea that I could write her a telegram telling her how much I loved her.

She got really spoiled that way. It got so bad that when I could afford it, I'd give her a nice diamond or something else. She'd take a look at it, then hand it back. I'd say, "Dolly, you don't like it?" She'd say, "Yes, I like it, but write something." She knew I'd write something telling her how much I loved her.

Anyway, I sat down to write the telegram. For some reason with the help of the good Lord, it was rhyming a little bit. I had never written a poem in my life. Finally, I thought—why not write a poem? So I worked on it all night long. The next morning it was finished. And I had told her, in verse, that I wouldn't be home on account of being snowbound and how much I loved her. Three days later I was back in the Valley. She threw her arms around me and told me how much she loved my telegram.

I forgot about it. After she was gone, our daughter, Betty, was straightening some things at the house one day and came across some special boxes. Dolly was very sentimental. She saved things like the very first Valentine I had sent her. All these things she had put away to keep. Betty found an envelope—across it was written IMPORTANT—FROM MY DARLING. Betty opened it and shook it out on the table. Dolly had read that telegram so many times it had fallen to pieces. This was in the day when you had the ribbon pasted on the paper. Betty had put it all together. I said, "That's the telegram I sent her from Des Moines, Iowa." Betty smiled, "Mother had it in writing." I said, "Okay."

A little while later we found one that I had written to her in 1956. Then I got an idea. Why not take a little book and put those with a picture of her family in it and maybe write some more in memory of her? I would give it to the family, even pass it on to the great-grandchildren who wouldn't know what a wonderful great-grandmother they had had. This way they would have firsthand information on the kind of person she had been.

So I did. I made this little book of poems. It turned out better than I had any right to expect. Our family and friends call it a treasure. And the idea came from that telegram sent from Des Moines in 1947.

> by Western Union
> from Des Moines, Iowa
> March 18, 1947
> our 27th anniversary
>
> To My Darling
>
> It was twenty-seven years ago
> And on this very day,
> I heard you speak those Precious words
> I had longed to hear you say.
>
> I was divinely happy then
> As everyone should know,
> With all your radiant beauty
> And because I loved you so.
>
> Your figure was blessed by the Fairies,
> Your lips were a cupid's bow,
> Your complexion shamed the lilies
> And your heart as pure as snow.

Tho your charms as a girl were unequaled,
So gorgeous and full of life,
They fade into naught by comparison
When I think of your charms as my Wife.

The years have enhanced your beauty
The sunbeams play in your hair,
Your eyes twinkle with laughter,
Broken hearts are mended there.

You are a marvelous mother
And still have the heart of a girl,
My love for you grows by the hour,
You still keep my head in a whirl.

Some day when this life is over
And I am laid to rest,
The world will continue to wonder
Why I was so wonderfully blessed.

And in the life beyond the grave
Where souls will never part,
I'll learn to my Eternal joy
You'll never leave my Heart.

      Lloyd

A GRAND BARBECUE AT KIAMICHI (THE 1950s)

Roy Buchannon worked for us at our ranch at Clarksville. He had a short fuse and steel blue eyes. He was tough. The story was that he had been in a few gunfights. Among his victims was his own father, who had a habit of getting drunk and beating up his wife and children. On several occasions when Roy was growing up, he had come to his mother's defense. As a reward he had been kicked or beaten into unconsciousness by his drunk father. After one such beating, he told his father to never beat his mother again—if he did, Roy would kill him. The next time Roy's father started to beat up his mother Roy, true to his word, went in and got his pistol and shot his dad.

While he was working for us on the Arrowhead Ranch at Clarksville, we acquired in a trade a 13,000-acre ranch in the Kiamichi Mountains of Oklahoma. Riding over the ranch, I noticed that it had been well fenced with a four-strand barbed wire fence, but at hundreds of places all four wires had been cut. In talking to the local people about this I was told that the mountaineers who lived around the ranch had had a falling out with the former owners and had framed the former owner's son on a cattle stealing charge. They had succeeded in having him sentenced to two years in the penitentiary. They had burned the residence on the ranch while the family was away from home. They had then cut the wire, which I had noticed. I was told that the mountaineers now considered the ranch open range and would burn up or destroy the fences if anyone attempted to rebuild them. While traveling over the ranch I saw hundreds of cattle, thereby verifying this story.

These same local residents told me that, as outsiders, we had no chance of stocking and using the ranch. I did not intend to give up 13,000 acres without a showdown. So when I went back to the Arrowhead Ranch at Clarksville, I told Roy Buchannon what the problem was. I asked him if he would consider becoming our foreman on this ranch and moving up there to rebuild the fences in hopes of stocking the ranch. He said, "I have just one question to ask. If I get in trouble, are you behind me all the way?" I told him that I was and that if he could anticipate any trouble coming to let me know. I would be right there with him to meet the trouble.

Roy moved to Kiamichi and began building the fences. Three or four of the local crowd, all carrying pistols, came up to visit where he and his men were working. They told Roy that the local people were going to keep this ranch as open range. The work they were doing was a waste of time and money. These same fellows would walk along with the fence builders and would try to impress them and Roy with their shooting ability by shooting their pistols at rocks and various objects. Since they were carrying their guns, Roy also carried his. He told me that one day, when it was unusually hot, he noticed a buzzard that was dropping down the side of the mountain. It was flying over where the men were working, then making a turn into the wind and heading back up the mountain. He said he watched the buzzard through the corner of his eye without seeming to pay any attention. He noticed that the buzzard virtually stopped over the workers as it turned back into the wind. He thought if he could time it exactly right he had a good chance of getting the buzzard as it seemed to stop in the air. Finally when he thought he had it, he drew his pistol and fired. To his and their surprise the buzzard tumbled to the ground dead.

Roy said, "After that, there was no more pistol practicing around my crew." A few days later the leader of the group asked if Roy would give him a job helping with the fencing. Roy said, "Yes, if you understand that if you draw our pay, you're on our team—all the way." The fellow agreed, and he and his two brothers became permanent employees.

As they began finishing the fence and closing up the gaps, I told Roy that we ought to have him invite the neighbors to a get-acquainted barbecue at the ranch headquarters. I told him to get the invitations out and to let me know how many might be at the barbecue. A few days later he told me there would probably be three to four hundred. Heretofore we had heard that the people living on one side of the mountain range in this area were feuding with the people living on the other side. But all had agreed to come to our barbecue.

I told Roy we would prepare food for three hundred at the Arrowhead Ranch at Clarksville and drive it to Kiamichi. But we would have no beer or liquor of any kind to try and avoid feuding troubles among the guests.

We did wind up with approximately three hundred guests. After the meal had been served, one of the local people, who claimed he was a judge, got up and thanked the people from Texas for a grand barbecue and a grand time. He said, "We want the Texas people to feel welcome to our area. You have done the local community a fine service. There has been considerable feuding between the people on either side of the mountain. This barbecue has brought us together and made us realize we're all pretty nice people after all. We've just been neglecting each other."

A few days later Roy told the locals that we were going to close the gap and we would appreciate them getting the cattle off the ranch. This, of course, was the acid test. Almost twenty cowboys appeared on horseback the next morning. They gathered and sold at public auction approximately 1,300 head of cattle.

We had a barbecue each year for the next several years. We had a fine relationship as long as we owned the ranch.

Several years later, I was contacted by a man in North Texas who wanted to buy this ranch. I told him our experience. I wanted him to know before we made a deal. He said, "That doesn't worry me. I have two hard-fisted sons who would welcome the excitement." I warned him that he was underestimating the situation. "You should consider keeping Roy as a permanent foreman. He has been accepted by the local people. He is probably the only man I know who can handle the job without problems." He paid little attention to what I told him, but he did give Roy the job.

About two years later Roy walked into my office and told me that the new owners had terminated his services about three months earlier.

While Roy had been at the ranch, one of the sons had moved into the residence at the headquarters. The other son had built an equally nice home close by. Within thirty days after Roy's services had been terminated, both houses had been burned to the ground. The wires had been cut in hundreds of places. The ranch was again open range.

I told Roy that he had done a great job for us. I was sorry for the other people's problems, but they had certainly been warned. I wanted Roy to know that he always had a job with us. He said, "Lloyd, I already have a job that I like very well. You know that I have a short fuse and am a little difficult to get along with. But on this job I am actually looking after five thousand people. And in all the time I have been there I have not had back talk or criticism from a single one of them." I questioned, "Where is this job, and what are you doing?" Roy smiled, "This job is in Dallas, and I'm managing a cemetery."

FIVE SPECKLED BELLIES ON A KNOLL (1950)

Elmer and I were hunting geese on the coast. We had climbed a knoll that was a little higher than the surrounding territory. We were trying to pick a location that would give us the best chance to shoot both ducks and geese. About a half mile to the north of us was a small lake. A man was standing on the bank of this lake.

A large flock of snow geese was drifting west from the coast about midway from where we were standing and the little lake. This man stepped under a small bush or tree and blew a goose call. There were at least a hundred geese in the flock. They made a right turn and headed directly for the lake. Time proved that he was shooting a pump gun. As the geese came in close, he fired and the leader fell. It was early in the season. The rest of the geese became excited and tried to follow the leader. He fired five more shells into the flock and not a goose fell, but each time he fired there were a dozen geese within twenty or thirty feet in front of him. He reloaded and fired five more shells before the geese were out of range. Again not a single goose fell. Elmer said, "That guy needs some help. Let's go down there." I answered, "No, I'm going to stay here a little while longer because I think this is a very good spot."

Elmer walked down off the knoll and headed for the lake through the low scattered brush. He had not been gone over two or three minutes when I saw five speckled bellies heading west about a quarter of a mile south of me. I was well covered by the low brush. Again our friend on the lake blew his goose call, and these speckled bellies heard it. They made a right turn and headed straight across my knoll. I stood quietly under the brush. They were flying not over twenty feet high and coming directly overhead. They were so close I didn't want to fire and tear them to pieces. So I grabbed my hunting cap and crept out from under the brush. I let out a loud war whoop and swung my hunting cap straight up at them. They stood on their tails and started to climb. When I thought they had gained sufficient distance, I started on the farthest speckled belly to the left, fired five times, and five geese lay on the knoll.

Elmer called, "What the hell are you shootin' at?" I answered, "Come and see." He called again, "No, tell me." I repeated, "You had better come and look." He walked back. I had taken my five speckled bellies and laid them side by side, belly up. As he climbed up on the knoll and saw them lying there, he said, "This is a hell of a note. I wasn't gone five minutes."

I laughed, "Elmer, it really didn't make any difference. There were only five of them. I didn't need any help." He didn't appreciate the joke.

"THIS IS JIMMY HOFFA" (1959)

In January 1959, a Valley family we will call the Smiths purchased approximately 2,700 acres of land out of the Jackson pasture. The land was newly cleared and the irrigation system recently built. For four or five years conditions were good and the payments met regularly. When Mr. Smith died, the burden of bad days plus a couple of bad years put them in a terrible bind for cash flow for payments and operating expenses.

About that time I received a telephone call. The party calling said, "This is Jimmy Hoffa." I was on the verge of saying "This is the Prince of Wales" when he said, "I understand that you are a banker in the Rio Grande Valley. If this is correct, I want to ask you if the Smiths bank with you and are they honest?" I told him they were an honest, capable, hardworking family, but conditions had got them in trouble financially. He thanked me for the information.

A week later the Smiths were in my office. They told me that they had been approached by the Teamsters offering to loan them money. The Teamsters wanted the Smiths to put their land as collateral so they would have first lien and they would pay off our notes. This all happened according to schedule and the loan was closed. Conditions continued to worsen from the standpoint of prices and within two or three years the Smiths could not make the payments. They told me that the Teamsters were going to foreclose on them and probably take judgment against their losses or any deficiency. Since the property would be sold on a low cash basis, it was entirely possible that, even though the property had the value in excess of the loan, on a cash basis it would not bring enough to pay the indebtedness in full.

A few days after this conversation, the Smiths called me and told me that a group of Teamsters was in the Valley and that their property was going to be sold the following Tuesday. The Teamsters had refused their offer and were going to try to attach Mrs. Smith Sr.'s inheritance in Mississippi. The Smiths told me that the value of this property was approximately $200,000. They wanted to save this property for their mother because it was all she had. I told the Smiths that we ought to get the property out of her name and that if they thought it was worth $200,000. I would pay them that figure and she could convey it to me. It would be a bona fide sale. Therefore, I did not think the Teamsters could get this property. If Mrs. Smith wanted, she would be paid in cash (which she was) or she could cash my check and put the money temporarily in bond or a locked box. This was accomplished and the deed filed of record in Mississippi.

Apparently the Teamsters left and went to Mississippi, where they found out that I had the deed on the property. They came back to the Valley and proceeded with the foreclosure. The Smiths told me that the Teamsters were very arrogant and unreasonable and they could do nothing with them. They asked me if I would sit in on the conversation the following evening. I told them that it might be a good idea for them to tell the Teamsters that I would invite the Smiths and the Teamsters to a dinner at Arrowhead Ranch. After dinner we would try to work out a solution.

When I met the three representatives at the ranch for dinner they were very arrogant and uncooperative. We served enchiladas buffet style. Dolly and I, the Smiths, and three representatives of the Teamsters Union comprised the dinner party. Each of these three men was about six feet tall and weighed about 230-240 pounds. They appeared to be in excellent physical condition. Dolly supervised the serving of the food at the buffet. Everyone took the seat assigned to him, but one took the seat Dolly usually occupied at the head of the table. I was already irritated by their attitude, and this irritated me even more. I walked down to where he was and told him that he was sitting in Mrs. Bentsen's chair and that I would appreciate him taking the chair assigned to him. He glared at me for fifteen or twenty seconds, then grabbed his plate and went into the living room to eat by himself. One of the others was sitting to my left at the table. At that time there had been a lot of unfavorable publicity against the Teamsters for riding roughshod over many organizations, for the slowdown in business, and for strikes. A lot of corruption within the Teamsters was then under investigation. The fellow sitting on my left asked my opinion of a certain strike that had gained a lot of notoriety because of the brutality against would-be workers. Being already at the boiling point from the previous incidents that had happened, I did not use very good language. I turned to the man and said, "You asked me so I will tell you. I don't know how you can satisfy a bunch of S.O.B.'s [and did not abbreviate] when all they want is more." He glared at me for about half a minute, grabbed his plate, and joined his associate in the living room to finish his dinner.

After dinner was over we all moved into the living room. Things could not have been going worse than they were. I told the group, including the Smiths, that they were not getting along very well and I was going to express my opinion of what I thought should be done and hoped to do so without interruption. Then I would, in turn, be willing to listen without interruption to any interested party. I hoped everyone would give each party their uninterrupted attention. I told them that the property they were foreclosing on was worth more than the Teamsters had inventoried it and could be sold for more money than the Smiths owed them. I told them that people do not look very favorably on people like the Smiths being taken advantage of by an organization such as the Teamsters who had already received a lot of bad publicity. This would certainly make it a great deal worse. Therefore, I recommended that the Smiths execute a deed to the property securing the total lien and that the Teamsters in turn accept the same in full satisfaction of the debt and there would be no unfavorable publicity. This was abruptly turned down by the Teamsters group. They in turn told me that as soon as the sale was over, if it did not bring enough on a cash sale to pay the debt in full, including all penalties and expenses, plus 10 percent attorney's fees on the entire loan, they were going to foreclose against the signature of the note for any deficiency and told me to consider that their final statement.

I excused myself and went into an adjoining room. I put in a call to a number Jimmy Hoffa had given me. I told him what had transpired and reiterated what I had suggested as a compromise, calling his attention to recent negative publicity and to the results of what he had in mind. He asked me if I thought the property involved was worth the amount of their loan. I told him that it not only was, but it had great potential for much further appreciation as soon as things came back to normal. He thanked me for calling him and told me the Teamsters would accept the property as payment and asked me to advise his representatives. I told him he had better hang on because I did not think they would take my word for the content of our conversation or believe that I had been talking to him personally.

    I went back into the living room and apologized for having to leave. I told the group how we were going to settle the transaction. My statement was immediately rejected by one of the Teamsters. He told me that I was not making the decisions. I told him that I had just talked to Jimmy Hoffa and what the results of my conversation with him had been. They were completely shocked and one of them said "Are you telling us that you talked to Jimmy Hoffa just now?" I told him "Yes," and that Hoffa was hanging on the telephone to give them the same message. The leader of the group rushed into the other room. The only part of the conversation that we heard was "Hello, but Mr. Hoffa, but"—and a pause, then buts continued for about two minutes and finally—"All right, Mr. Hoffa, if you say so." He came back into the room and said that he had talked to Mr. Hoffa and that he had agreed. The deal was closed in this manner.

    The aftermath of the Mississippi property was that in about sixty days a party called me from Mississippi and asked me if I cared to sell the property. I told him that I would call him back but that I wanted to know what he would pay for it. His offer was as I recall some thirty-five to forty thousand dollars more than I had paid for it. We closed the transaction and I sent a check to the Smiths for the profit I had made on the sale. They said, "We are not entitled to this, you bought the property, it's yours." I said, "No, I went into the deal to help you in a crisis, and I made a profit. This money belongs to your mother and I want her to have it."

    Needless to say, this was the only contact I ever had with Jimmy Hoffa.

"RUN!" (1960)

We had bought a number of ranches in East Texas, one of them located near a little settlement called Cut Hands. This ranch had been purchased on "walk out" basis, which meant cattle, equipment, everything went with the ranch. The cattle were not the quality we wanted, but since at this time the market was not good, we decided to leave them on the ranch for the time being. They would pick up a little weight as the grass improved in the spring and, probably, the price would be better. But the cattle had to be worked and branded. Some of them were "keepable" and others were not. So we began sorting them in the corrals and sending them to various pastures. In other words, shaping them up.

I was working in the triangle pen at the head of the chute and instructing the men on the cutting gates, by sign, as to which tract they would be turned into. Of course, these were wild cattle. I was watching them closely so, if need be, I could jump to the top of the chute, which was made of heavy pine board. I could climb it in a hurry. A two-year-old black bull of inferior quality was moving ahead toward the cutting gates. He whirled to attack me! This bull was a little quicker than most, or I had not started soon enough. He caught my left leg with his head against the corral. He was strong enough and big enough that he could quickly break a leg. It all happened so fast! When I saw I couldn't pull my leg loose, I threw my right leg over his back. It startled him, and he released my left leg, which was what I hoped he would do. The bull wasn't the only one startled. So was the man on the cutting gates who, instead of closing the gates so that I could jump to one or the other side of the chute, left a cutting gate open. The result? The bull dove through the opening with me on his back. In a split second we were in the middle of the large trap. He leaped and bucked. I knew it would be only seconds until I would be on the ground and the bull on top of me.

Remembering my early years bulldogging steers, I leaned forward and put my elbows on the top of his head. I reached my left hand over and caught as near the tip of his horn as I could and dropped my right hand to throw him. But my hand slipped and I caught his lower jaw right up close to his front teeth. This was a lucky maneuver and actually worked better. I threw my entire weight to the left, twisted his neck and, in a flash, he was on his back in the middle of the corral, with his long horns helping me hold him down. I had hold of his jaw and wouldn't let him turn his head. In seconds my cowboys had leaped into the corral and thrown their ropes to his hind legs. With a rope on each side that bull could not get up.

I was furious. His quality being so poor, I told my cowboys to castrate him, which they did. I continued to hold his head on the ground. The boys had their ropes on his front and hind legs so he could not roll over. He kept struggling, snorting, and bellowing, and his disposition grew worse.

Two black city teenagers who had seen the corrals, which were close to the road, had stopped to watch us work the cattle. I paid no attention to them. They were dressed in their zoot suits, popular at the time. They seemed to be interested in what was going on with the bull.

I told the cowboys, "We have to turn this bull loose. So remove your ropes as quiet as you can. I'll release my hands from his horns . . . easy . . . we'll make it to the edge of the corral before he knows he's loose." The bull, thinking he was tied, was perfectly still. We all jumped onto the top of the corral on a run. Then I saw that the two teenagers had come inside the corral and were standing there staring at the bull. Right about then the bull realized he was loose. I screamed at them to run, and they realized they had waited too long. They headed for the side of the corral, about nine hundred feet away.

The bull leaped to his feet, let out two terrific roars and leaped straight up and down as he was swinging his head around. He spotted the two teenagers streaking for the corral fence, one directly behind the other. The one in front was running at top speed facing the corral. The second one was running directly behind him reaching for the fence but turning around, only to see the bull coming at top speed. The first teenager hit the corral fence and started to climb. The second one started to climb right after him. Just as they reached the top of the corral fence, the bull hit the boards just under their feet, and they fell over on the opposite side of the fence. It was a sight to see.

Once we realized no one was really hurt, everyone doubled over with laughter. I think those teenagers lost 90 percent of their curiosity.

A LITTLE MORE POWDER WILL DO A LOT BETTER JOB (1960)

I had acquired some loading equipment for both shotguns and rifles. My old book of directions was outdated for modern powder. Nevertheless, I used it for a guide and began loading shotgun shells for the hunting season.

Lloyd Jr. and I had decided to go quail hunting, and I didn't tell him that my shells had a super charge. I figured if I wanted more distance, just add a little more powder, which I had done. It was late in the season and the quail had been hunted a lot. They were quite wild.

We had gotten out of the car and walked a short distance when a covey of quail took off. They were out of shotgun range, but I leveled down on them, pulled the trigger, and one fell. Lloyd Jr. had not even raised his gun. He complimented me on the shot. Then he laughed and asked if I was using a shotgun or a rifle. We walked over and picked up the quail, then walked a short distance farther. Again the quail took off out of range. I raised my gun, picked out a quail, pulled the trigger, and it fell. Lloyd Jr. said, "Dad, I have never seen a shotgun shoot that far. What kind of shells are you using?" I told him they were some that I had loaded myself and that I had "souped them up" a little. He replied, "You hunt by yourself. I want more distance. I don't want to be around those shells." Then I noticed that the casing was completely shattered. I had to dig it out with my knife. So I decided to discontinue using paper shells. I went entirely to plastic because they would not shatter.

Several weeks later we were hunting in Mexico. In the forenoon I was using a 20-gauge shotgun. The birds were plentiful, but because of a high wind they were flying extremely high. After eating lunch I decided to switch to a 12-gauge. I had learned never to go hunting with more than one size shell in my hunting jacket, so I proceeded to empty the 20-gauge shells out of my jacket and replace them with the 12-gauge shells. But in the field I had no place to put the 20-gauge shells. So I decided to put them in the left pocket of my hunting jacket and to carry the 12-gauge shells in my right pocket. Birds began flying and were extremely high. With the super loaded shells I was showing off a little by making shots that everyone thought completely out of range. I was quite proud of my success in loading shotgun shells.

All of a sudden a flock flew over. When I pulled the trigger, my gun clicked. I presumed one of my shells had misfired. I opened the gun. It was an automatic, and there was no empty casing in the shotgun. So I thought the gun had simply missed a shell. I injected another shell, and as the birds flew over I fired. There was a tremendous racket and recoil of the shotgun—so much so that my head ached and I had a roaring in my ears. Then I looked at my shotgun. About halfway up, the barrel was the size of a large cantaloupe. Evidently, the barrel had "stretched" instead of bursting. Then I realized what had happened. In the rush of reloading for the birds, I had grabbed a 20-gauge shell and put it in the gun. When I pulled the trigger, the firing arm had pushed it up in the barrel. It was one of the super loaded shells. I learned later there was only one shotgun barrel that would take that kind of punishment. I was glad I was shooting one of them.

A short time later, Dolly and I were driving across Arrowhead Ranch. I had again been loading my rifle shells. I was shooting a 220 Swift. As we drove by, I saw a large covey of quail on the bare ground under a mesquite tree about 300 yards from the road. Then I noticed a hawk sitting up in the tree above the quail, looking them over. I stopped the car, dropped the window, and put my rifle out the window. I told Dolly I was going to kill that hawk before he had a banquet of quail.

When I would fire my rifle from the car, Dolly would always lean over behind me and put her fingers in both ears to keep out the pressure. I drew a bead on the hawk and squeezed the trigger.

I thought the car had exploded! It almost had! The bullet had blown out of the rifle. The thing that saved me was that, sitting in the car, I had to stoop over to see through the scope. The bullet went out under my chin and out the angel-wing of the car. The recoil had burst both my eardrums. Dolly was saved by being behind me with her fingers in her ears.

At first I was stunned and didn't realize what had happened to the rifle, thinking maybe the bullet had stuck in the barrel. I got out of the car and walked over to the mesquite tree. The hawk was lying on the ground dead so I knew the bullet had left the barrel.

I contacted the company that had made the rifle and told them the experience. They said that several years earlier they had discontinued the manufacture of the 220 Swift. They had discovered that the normal Wildcat with the proper load would build up pressure of 20,000 to 24,000 pounds in the chamber with each shell fired. But the 220 Swift would build up to about 50,000 pounds. If you used only a very small increase of powder over the recommended mixture, it became the equivalent of a bomb.

It was one way of convincing me to get a modern, up-to-date book of directions. And I picked up a little religion on doing things the way the book said they should be done instead of "a little more powder would do a lot better job."

DAD'S BLACKBERRY JAM (1962)

The area around Clarksville, Texas, and along the Red River, was one of the earliest parts of the state settled by immigrants moving in from the East and from Georgia and Tennessee.

The land was cleared of timber. It was ideal for cattle, corn, hay, cotton, and many varieties of fruit and berries. Generally the area was settled in medium size farms, eighty acres or larger. The size of the farm depended a lot on the number of slaves or the size of the family the settler had. Years went on. During the Depression cattle prices along with grain and corn prices dropped so low that it was no longer possible to make a profit. A lot of these farms could be had at a very low figure. People moved off the farms. Buildings and improvements built in more prosperous times were abandoned, in many cases destroyed by time, wind, and weather, as well as by fire.

Years had passed when we became interested in the area. We were able to buy many of the farms and build ranches of sufficient size to afford management and to make them profitable. One of these ranches we named the Arrowhead at Clarksville. It was a beautiful ranch, joining the Red River. We rehabilitated one of the nicest sets of buildings and made it our headquarters.

The ranch was covered with beautiful pecan trees and other timber, especially in the lowland. One day when we were working cattle, I was impressed by the fact that whenever we rode by one of the abandoned home sites, the fruit trees that had been planted in earlier years were loaded with pears, plums, and persimmons. The blackberry vines were loaded with luscious blackberries as big as the end of your thumb. These vines were in bunches as high as the back of your horse. I asked my foreman what they did with all that beautiful fruit. He said, "Nothing. We put up a little of it to take care of our needs. The rest of it goes to waste." I said, "Jay, I grew up in hard country. My dad and mother were immigrants. One of the things we were taught was to never let anything go to waste. I wish you would tell some of your men to pass the word to families living on the ranch and adjacent to the ranch that we will pay $1 a bushel for all the blackberries they can pick tomorrow." He said, "All right."

The next day we worked cattle all day. That evening as we rode our horses by the ranch house, I looked over on the porch. There were probably thirty-five to forty bushel baskets, every one of them heaped high with blackberries. Jay laughed. "Mr. Lloyd, what are you going to do with all those blackberries?" I answered, "Let me do some figuring. I don't intend to let them go to waste." My mother had taught her children not only to be conservative but also how to care for and preserve food. That included blackberry jam. I knew the process but not the ingredients, so I called my daughter, Betty, in McAllen. She called back with a recipe. She said that she couldn't wait to taste "Dad's blackberry jam." Now I was ready. I told Jay, "Take the pickup and go into Clarksville and bring a ton of sugar." I listed the other ingredients I would need along with the approximate quantities. I told him the number of glass jars we would need in pints, quarts, and half-gallons. It took a lot to accommodate the amount of jam that I thought we could make from the supply of berries we had on hand.

We filled barrels with water and dumped several baskets of blackberries in each barrel. As we poured the berries slowly into the water, the leaves and trash would float to the top. As the berries began to fill the barrel, the water would rise and carry the trash over the edge of the barrel. Then we dipped the clean berries out of the barrels and put them in large containers. Fortunately, we had an annual barbecue at the ranch and consequently had large cooking vessels on hand. We began cooking the berries, putting each cowboy on one large cooker to constantly stir the berries until the jam was ready to receive the sugar and go into the jars. Jay finally arrived with the sugar and jars, telling me he had had to go to three towns to get enough to fill the order.

When the sun came up the following morning, we had thirty-six cases of jars of the most delicious blackberry jam. We had to use the pickup to transport it to the Valley. I became quite popular giving away this luscious blackberry jam over the next year's time. We men had been stirring jam all night and putting it in jars. As we sat down to breakfast, my foreman said, "We're not going to work cattle today, are we?" I said, "Certainly we are. We have to finish the job." So we worked cattle all day. The following morning when we left to come back to the Valley, my foreman remarked, "Mr. Lloyd, we're sure all glad to see you come, but I think there is a possibility that my boys are also glad to see you go."

THIS COW HAD A PERMANENT GRUDGE (ABOUT 1964)

We were working cattle on the Arrowhead at Clarksville. I was in the working pens so that I could classify them better. These were wild cattle. You had to be very careful because often they would pass within one to three feet of you. They would whirl to attack. You had to be ready to leap to the top of the corral fence at any time.

In an instant one of these cows whirled and knocked me to the ground. Ordinarily when this happened, the cow would whirl around and go out of the corral. This cow evidently had a permanent grudge because she had no such intention.

Realizing I was alone and that it would be over in moments, I had to somehow get out of that corral. So with her hooking me and fighting, I pulled myself to the top of the corral fence, board by board, with the cow butting me all the way. By the time I reached the top of the corral and threw myself over on the other side, my men were able to come to my assistance, but it was too late. I tried to get up, then realized my leg was broken.

I told the foreman to get his pickup. We headed for the hospital in Clarksville. I held my broken leg in my hands over ten miles of rough road. He drove the pickup wide open. By the time we had gotten to the hospital, the pain was quite intense. They carried me into the hospital on a stretcher. I was bruised black and blue from my shoulders down. The entire leg from the middle of the thigh down had turned almost black and had swollen to about twice its normal size. The doctors took one look at it and told me, "You have internal hemorrhaging. We won't touch it. The nearest place that could possibly help you would be Texarkana, sixty-five miles away." They said, "We'll give you an injection that will help stop the hemorrhage by coagulating the blood. We'll give you another injection to ease the pain." They did.

I asked them to let me sit in a wheelchair so I could get to a telephone. I put in a call to Lloyd Jr. because he had our plane and had gone to a football game in Dallas. Fortunately, they located him in the hotel just before the game. I told him, "Lloyd, I want you to send the plane to Clarksville as quick as you can. I had a bout with a cow and came out second best. Among other things, she broke my right leg." He said, "Dad, the plane is in the shop having some work done on the engine. I doubt it's ready to go, but I have a friend sitting by me who has a plane. He will send it right away, but where can he land?" It was decided that the plane could not land on the strip in Clarksville. We would meet the plane in Paris, Texas, about twenty miles away. Again, we took the pickup. We met the plane in Paris and flew to Houston where the ambulance was waiting.

Dolly was there to meet me—she had stayed in Houston while I was in Clarksville working cattle on the ranch. I don't believe I had ever seen her so pale in my life as she was when they placed me on the stretcher and carried me to Methodist Hospital. They completed their examinations very quickly. The doctor said, "Our first problem is to stop the internal bleeding. If we are successful in this, in two or three days, we will set the bone. There is a very potent possibility that this leg will have to be amputated." I looked quickly at Dolly to see if she heard. She had. I thought she was going to faint. I told her not to worry, that I healed quickly, and everything would be all right. Then I turned to the doctor and said, "Doctor, I don't think I am interested in what you said." He questioned, "Meaning what?" I answered, "I have had broken bones before and I don't want to wait three days for this leg to start healing. I want you to set it now." The doctor said, "With this tremendous swelling we cannot. We have got to get the swelling down before your leg can be set." I said, "You may be right, Doctor, but before making that decision, I want you to try first and see whether you can set it or not." He answered, "I suppose I could give you a sedative and try to set it. I doubt if it will work." The doctor did try. He was the finest orthopedic surgeon in Houston. In surgery the bones snapped into place. I was in the hospital three days. Then I was moved to the Valley wearing a heavy cast from the thigh to the ankle.

A couple of weeks from the day I arrived home I became restless. I knew that my cowboys were working cattle on the Rincón Ranch. Dolly had gone to town, so I was alone at home. I used my crutches to walk out to the car. I left Dolly a note that I would be back in two hours and drove to Rincón. Following the trails across the ranch, I came to one of the corrals where there had been a lot of activity. I stopped my car. Then I could hear the cattle coming through the brush and the cowboys rounding up the cattle heading them toward the corral. A trap adjacent to the corral had a gate on the north side and a gate on the west side. Both gates had been left open because they were not certain which direction the herd would come, but now it was obvious they were coming in the west gate. Realizing that the cattle knew where both gates were, I realized that when they came in the west gate, the cattle would head on a dead run to get out the north gate. So I turned my car around and drove to the north gate, hoping to stop the cattle from going out that way.

About that time the leader of the cows came through the west gate on a dead run. I realized having my car by the gate would not stop these wild cattle. The gate had to be closed, and it had to be done in seconds. I grabbed my crutches, opened the door, and ran to grab the gate. But holding one crutch in each hand and attempting to close the gate was a little slow. And these cows were coming!

The lead cow saw what I was trying to do. Instead of heading for the gate, she headed for me. I was at least fifteen feet from my car—and on crutches! I gave the gate a shove, and it swung closed. The cow was almost on top of me. I dropped the crutches and ran to the opposite side of the car with the cast on my leg. I was not supposed to put any weight on my leg at all, but I had no other choice. I had very frightening thoughts that I might have injured the leg. I was mad at myself for getting in this kind of predicament in the condition I was in. But I also realized that my leg was not hurting at all. The cowboys rode up and put the chain on the north gate. I drove my car out the west gate and they closed it up. Still a little surprised that my leg had not bothered me, I got out of the car and carefully put a little weight on the leg. It seemed to me that it was entirely solid, but, of course, it had the cast on it. I got in the car and drove home.

Dolly was waiting for me and was very annoyed that I had taken the car and driven off by myself, but glad to see that I wasn't hurt. I did not tell her about the incident. The principal worry I had when this cow was after me was that if anything happened to my leg, my doctor in Houston would not only give me the devil for getting into such a predicament, but might also insist I have my head examined. The next morning I called my doctor in Houston. I did not tell him what had happened, but I did tell him that I had been putting a little weight on the leg and that it seemed to be entirely solid. I carefully evaded telling him I had already made a hundred-yard dash. He said, "You have not had sufficient time. Your leg could not possibly be that far along. But if you want to, go see Dr. Reidland in McAllen. He is a bone specialist. See what he says." I did see Ken Reidland. He X-rayed my leg, then picked up the phone, and called the doctor in Houston. He said the bone appeared to be entirely solid. The Houston doctor authorized Dr. Reidland to remove the cast and cautioned me to use the crutches for another two weeks. I started putting weight on my leg the rest of that day. The next day Ken Reidland reduced the two-week order to two days. I threw away the crutches.

DANISH LULLABIES (THE 1980s)

One day I received a letter from Denmark. The writer said he was probably a second cousin of mine. He and his wife wanted to make a trip to the United States and see the Texas branch of the Bentsen family, which began, of course, with my father and mother. He stated that the letter was being written for him by his niece, who taught the English language. Primarily he wanted to know whether I spoke Danish, because neither he nor his wife spoke English. I wrote back and told him that I did not speak Danish, but that would not be a problem. When they came, I wanted them to spend as much time as they liked in our home, I would loan them a car to tour whatever portions of the United States they wanted to see, and I would get an interpreter who would stay in our home as long as they were here so that we could carry on a normal conversation. We made arrangements with a professor at the University of Texas who spoke Danish.

One evening we invited the cousins (Knud and Sidse), the interpreter, Don and Nell, and Betty and Dan to have dinner at Pelican's Wharf in McAllen. During the evening's conversation, we would talk through the interpreter. He would explain our remarks to them and theirs to us. I was hearing more of the Danish language than I had ever heard. Then the interpreter turned and said something to Knud using a word that sounded like "krage." I recognized the word as meaning "crow." I held up my hand and said, "Wait a minute. I think I remember something." I began to sing a song in Danish. As soon as I started, the professor and the cousins joined me in the song and we sang it through. I remembered both the words in Danish and the tune! I again held up my hand and said, "I remember something else." I began to sing another tune and the words came to my mind, all in the Danish language. They again joined in with me and sang it all the way through. We were all astounded, and I said, "What on earth was I singing?" They laughed and said the two songs I sang are the songs a Danish mother sings to her baby when she rocks the baby to sleep. Something had unlocked a memory in my mind that must have happened when I was two or three years old.

My mother felt so strongly about her children being what she called "100 percent American" and speaking without a Danish accent that she and Pop, after having been founding members of the Lutheran Church in White, South Dakota, left the church because the Lutheran minister conducted the service in Danish. In the same year they were cofounders of the Methodist Church in White, South Dakota, where it was stipulated the service be conducted in English. Yet, surely, mothers rocking their babies to sleep do have special privileges.

"HOW CAN A SILVER DOLLAR EVER BE WORTH LESS THAN A DOLLAR?" (1930-1987)

When Edna and I had been married about ten years, I got the idea that I wanted to start a coin collection. I started gathering old coins. I would bring them home and would try to clean them. Coin collector friends said, "You can't clean these coins. You'll destroy all their value." I said, "I don't want these dirty coins around." "You better leave them," they warned. Luckily I listened. I was destroying their value by making them look pretty. In those days they weren't very expensive so we built up a bigger and bigger gold coin collection.

One day I said, "Edna, I'm going to put together a silver collection, too." So I would go to the bank where they would get bags of five hundred silver dollars. The bank would call me if they had a bag with a lot of uncertain coins in it. I would give them $500. I would come home and work half the night, picking out the coins from the five hundred that I wanted to add to my collection. Then I would take the rest of them back to the bank. I would sell them the ones I didn't want for $1—the same I had paid for them. I finally ended up with 12,787 silver dollars. They were seven complete sets of every silver dollar that had ever been struck. And they cost me $12,787. Every once in a while Edna would tell me, "Don't you think you're spending too much money on these coins?" I would say, "Dolly, how can a silver dollar ever be worth less than a dollar?" She would answer, "Oh, all right." I think she thought I was spending too much time with them and not enough time with her.

Some time later, about 1975, a fellow called from Florida and asked permission to come down and look at my coin collection. I had long since moved it to the McAllen Bank because Edna had become worried about me keeping it at home. Too many people knew where I had it. We put a big story in the paper when we moved it. It was critical that people know it was in the bank. Anyway, this man from Florida arrived. I took him to the bank vault and, as we went over the silver collection, he became very excited. I told him I wouldn't sell the gold collection. (At that time some of the coins were worth $15,000 and $20,000 each. He asked, "You want to sell the silver collection?" I answered, "Well, you could make me an offer. It cost me $12,787. I would be interested in knowing how much your offer is." He said, "$1,000.000." I said, "You don't mean it." He said, "I do." I said, "Well, I'm not going to sell them."

Editor's Note

One day in the fall of 1986 Dad told me he had decided to sell his coins. After I told him what a bad idea I thought that was, he replied, "Well, if you thought it was a good idea, how would you go about it? You see, honey, I won't live forever. And you four children will have to deal with it. One of you will say, 'Give it to a national museum.' Another will say, 'A state museum.' A third will say, 'Divide the coins among the family.' And a fourth will say, 'Sell the coins and divide the money among the family.' All good ideas, but I'm going to save you all that trouble." Dad had become an accomplished numismatist and for more than fifty years had studied and collected those coins.

The May 1987 auction was held at Sotheby's in New York City. The Sotheby's catalog devoted entirely to Dad's coins listed the sale in three sessions, two gold and one silver. Dad, instead of sitting upstairs in the "seller's" secluded chair, chose to be right down on the floor, taking note of the selling price of each coin. The return was handsome. Dad was pleased.

Following the sale, a stranger who had bought a few of the coins approached Dad, whose name had not appeared in any of the literature. "It was your collection, wasn't it?" the man asked. When Dad smiled, the man shook his hand heartily and said, "Mazel tov!"

WORDS OF WISDOM

Two young men were walking along a road. Each noticed a small sparkle in the dust. The first thought it might be a grain of sand turned just right to catch the rays of the sun and passed on. The second wanted to know if it was "opportunity," so he stepped aside and uncovered a gem of great value.

In like manner words of wisdom come to our ears daily. Some listen and profit, others scarcely notice. The Bible says that some seed falls on fertile ground and some falls by the wayside.

Many years ago I saw "the girl of my dreams," certainly the epitome of feminine loveliness, charm, and beauty. I realized my shortcomings and that I had very little to offer, but I was also romantic enough to know she was the one and only and without her there was no future. I felt inadequate and lost, then I remembered the words of wisdom, "Faint heart ne'er won fair lady." And I began a campaign that culminated in fifty-eight years of happiness beyond my fondest dreams, so much so that the grandeur of heaven as my mother pictured it to me had to lose some of its appeal because I had the blessings of heaven on earth. The above shows how words of wisdom can lead to happiness. Now let me also relate how they can apply to success.

A little over a hundred years ago my father and mother immigrated to America from Denmark. In those days the poor crossed on cattle boats because it was cheaper and they could pay part of the cost by working. The trip took twenty-seven days and because of the confinement and hardship many died and were buried at sea. The reason for the trip was to own a piece of land you could call your own, something unheard of in Denmark, where land was so precious it was not sold but kept in the hands of the landed gentry, "the wealthy." They had heard that America had surplus land and wanted it settled and would give a hundred and sixty acres to those who would cultivate it and live on it for two years. My parents selected their land, dug a hole in the prairie because they had no money to build a house, covered the hole with timber and branches, covered that with straw and then sod. It served as their home until they could make enough to build a house. They plowed their land with a walking plow pulled with a horse and a cow. Later this same horse and cow, driven by my mother, pulled the reaper and my father tied the sheaves. Later when we had binders the sheaves were called bundles. I tell this story to show how precious land is to those who have none and no hopes of ever owning any.

My father and my mother used to tell me, "Lloyd, get hold of all the land you can and never part with it. Some day in your future this booming population will catch up with the surplus land and then you'll see what land is really worth and how precious it is." They also said land values can fluctuate short term due to a changing economy, but the general trend over the long term will always be upward because, as the population grows more and more, people will want to own a ranch, a farm, a garden. This is what has happened in the old countries and is happening here, and now looking back nearly a hundred years I see how sound their logic was. When they retired sixty years later the land that was worth a few cents an acre sold for $165 an acre and today it is double that figure at least. I personally think that city dwellers as well as rural look for the day they can own their own ranch, farm, hunting camp, or garden, just a piece of mother earth that is their very own. This creates the demand that helps push prices higher, and I have to say that I'm only calling your attention to what you already know.

People say I've had a wonderful life. I have. I think when I was born the Good Lord looked down and said, "This kid is going to need some extra help." I sure appreciate it.

Appendix

Lloyd Millard Bentsen was born in White, South Dakota, on November 24, 1893. He grew up on the stock farm his parents homesteaded when they immigrated to the United States from Denmark in the late 1800s.

His military service began when he enlisted during World War I. He served in the Aviation Section of the Signal Corps, United States Army. He was assigned to the 198th Aero Squadron, received his wings and his commission as an officer, and became a member of the "Flying Wildcats."

After World War I he moved to Mission, Texas, where he married Edna Ruth Colbath, who was from a pioneer Texas family. They had four children, Senator Lloyd Bentsen Jr., deceased; Donald Bentsen, deceased; Kenneth Bentsen, Houston; and Betty Bentsen Winn, McAllen. Mr. and Mrs. Bentsen had been married fifty-seven years at the time of her death. Their family always ranked foremost in their lives. His last Christmas was celebrated with forty-five children, grandchildren, and great-grandchildren at his home. He was a member of the First Baptist Church of McAllen. Along with many other philanthropies, he was a major supporter of the Rio Grande Children's Home, whose sport center was dedicated to the memory of Mrs. Bentsen. The Lloyd and Dolly Bentsen Elementary School in Sharyland is named in their honor.

Immediately prior to the outbreak of World War II, he organized and commanded a Texas Defense Guard battalion in the Rio Grande Valley, which sparked the organization of defense guard units all over Texas. He was inducted into the guard's Hall of Honor.

After serving thirteen years, he retired as commanding general of the Texas State Guard Reserve Corps and was recognized as "one of Texas' most distinguished citizen soldiers." The National Guard Association of Texas presented to him the "Minuteman Award," the association's highest award for distinguished service. In 1987 he was honored by the Texas Business Hall of Fame. In 1992 he was posthumously inducted as one of the first members of the Heritage Hall of Honor at the State Fair of Texas.

Among his other achievements he was cofounder of the Valley Chamber of Commerce and its first president; received the Silver Beaver Award from the Boy Scouts of America; was cofounder of the Mission–McAllen Beef Syndicate, which encourages young people to raise quality animals to be shown at livestock shows; co-donor of Bentsen State Park; cofounder of Lincoln Liberty Life Insurance Company; former member of the Texas Good Neighbor Commission; received the Marine Corps League Citation of Merit for loyalty to community and country; received Texas A&M University award to Outstanding Texans; was senior chairman of the board of Texas Commerce Bank, McAllen, after having served half a century as its chairman.

At ninety-five, he continued to manage his extensive ranching and farming operations as well as his real estate, oil, gas, and banking interests. He was an avid sportsman and co-organizer of the Valley Sportsman's Club, where he retained membership for more than half a century. Hunting and fishing were among his hobbies and ranged from the grizzlies and salmon of the Yukon to the snook and bonefish of Nicaragua.

Lloyd Bentsen passed away January 17, 1989.

Index

Page references in *italics* indicate photographs

A

Abraham, Joe, 110–111
accidents: fatal, xviii; motorcycle, xii, 38, *43*, 49–55; second broken leg, 158–161; shootings, 23–24, 28–30
Air Force. *See* Signal Corps
airplanes, xii–xiii, 63–67
A. J. Aubrey shotgun, 7–12
Alaska, *130*, 136–140
alcohol: investors and, xxiii; moonshine, 104–105; sobriety promise, xiii, 79
American Dream, 4
American Legion celebration, xiii, 78–80
amputation, threat of, 54, 159
anniversary poem, 141–143
Armistice Day, 69
Army Signal Corps. *See* Signal Corps
Arrowhead Ranch: dinner with Teamsters, 149–151; hunting at, 155–156
attacks on, 87–89, 90–91, 98–99
automobiles: as ambulance, 50; driving on ice, 31; driving speed, xi; of employees, 109–110; enlistment and, 56, 58–59; fatal accident, xviii; honeymoon, 81–82, 83; shooting from, 155–156; shot at by employee, 87–88. *See also* motorcycles
Aviation Mechanics Training Station, 65–67
awards and honors, 167–168

B

baby blue dress, 81–84
Baggus barn, 8
Baker, Mildred, 61, 79
Ballí, Beak, 97–99
Ballí, Fale, 97–99
Ballí, Paredes, 97–99
bank examiners, 103
banks: Elsa State Bank, xv; entering banking business, 100–103; First National Bank of Mission, xv, 103, 106–109; Texas Commerce Bank, 168. *See also* borrowing
barbecue, 145–146
barn dance, 38
Benson, Lieutenant, 63–65
Bentsen, Alton, xiii, *42*
Bentsen, B. A. (Beryl Ann), xxiv, 136
Bentsen, Betty. *See* Winn, Betty Bentsen
Bentsen, Carl. *See* Bentsen, Magnus
Bentsen, Dietz, *42*
Bentsen, Donald (son): in Chicago, 121–122; defending father, 109–110; entertaining investors, xxii; mentioned, xiii, xxi, 136, 162, 167; photographs of, *124*, *127*, *129*; watermelons and, 118; during World War II, xxiii, *127*
Bentsen, Edna (sister), *42*
Bentsen, Edna Colbath "Dolly" (wife): baby blue dress, 81–84; courtship, xii–xiii, 61, 62; dinner with Teamsters, 149–150; family, xxi, 75–77; with family, *124*, *126*, *127*, *128*; inheritance, 75–77; in labor conflicts, 87–88, 109–110; lack of domestic skills, 77; on Lloyd's coin collection, 163–164; on Lloyd's education, 69; Lloyd's second broken leg, 159–160, *161*; with Lyndon B. Johnson, *128*; marriage, xiii, 167; mentioned, 12, 136, 155; perfume, xxii; photograph of, *46*; poems to, xvii, 141–143; relationship with Lloyd, xvi, xvii, 76–77, 165; sobriety promise to, xiii, 79; in World War II, xxiii, *127*
Bentsen, Elmer (brother): apple "sampling," 35; Bentsen State Park, xv; double dating with, 62; goose hunting with, 147–148; guns and, 22–23, 23–24; vs. labor recruiters, 85–86; mentioned, xiii, xxii, 78; moonshine, 104–105; partnership with Lloyd, xiv, 103; photographs of, *42*

Bentsen, Kenneth (son): entertaining investors, xxii; mentioned, xiii, xxi, 136, 167; in photographs, *127*; during World War II, xxiii, *127*
Bentsen, Laurel, *42, 43*
Bentsen, Lloyd Millard III, xxiv, 136
Bentsen, Lloyd Millard Jr.: in Chicago, 121–122; on Dad's memoir, xxiv; entertaining investors, xxii; family photographs, *124, 127*; hunting with, *129, 130,* 154; in labor disputes, 87–89, 109–110; with Lyndon B. Johnson, *128*; mentioned, xiii, xxi, 79, 136, 159, 167; politics, xvii; watermelons and, 118; during World War II, xxiii, *127*
Bentsen, Lloyd Millard Sr., xxiv; Bentsen State Park, xv, *130*; birth of, xi, 167; business and (*See* banks; insurance; labor relations); courtship, xii–xiii, 61, 62; death of, xviii, 168; early years, xi–xii, 3–39, *40, 41, 42*; education, 19–24, *41*, 57, 68–69; family, xvi–xvii, *42, 127* (*See also* names of individual family members); as farm laborer, xi–xii, 6–7, 32; hunting (*See* hunting); land (*See* land); in later life, xi, *128,* 135–166; with Lyndon B. Johnson, *128*; marriage, xiii, 167; in middle years, 75–122, *123*; military service (*See* military service); motorcycle accident, xii, *43,* 49–55; parents (*See* Bentsen, Niels; Bentsen, Tena; parents); relationship with Dolly, xvi, xvii, 76–77, 81–84, 141–143, 165
Bentsen, Magnus: apple "sampling," 35; bent rifle barrel, 33–34; at Lake Ponsett, 36–37; opening coffins, 16–17
Bentsen, Mary, xxiv
Bentsen, Nell, xxiv, 162
Bentsen, Niels Peter (father): advice to Lloyd, 75, 100, 166; football, 19, 21; hunting at Black Slew (Oak Lake), 7–8, 11–12; immigration of, xi, 165–166; Lloyd's enlistment, 58–59; Lloyd's motorcycle accident, 51–52, 52–53; Magnus and, 33–34; mentioned, 30, 121; move to Texas, xiii; photographs of, *42, 43, 44*; union workers, 27, 28
Bentsen, Tena Petersen (mother): Americanization of children, xi, 163; Danish lullabies, 162–163; immigration of, xi, 4, 165–166; Lloyd's motorcycle accident, 51, 54; move to Mission, Texas, xi; photographs of, *42, 43*
Bentsen State Park, xv, *130,* 168
Black Slew, 7–12
blackberry jam, 156–158
blizzards, 5–6

Bohannan Cannery, 117
bone specialists, 54, 161
bone surgery, 54
books, favorites, 12
borrowing, 100–103
boxcars, riding, xii, 32
boxing: at county fair, 13–14; with employee, 87–89; with Ernest Mullins, 115–116; strategy, 31–33
broken leg: by cow, 158–161; enlistment and, 56–60; motorcycle accident, xii, 51–52; rebreaking of, xii, 52–55
Brookings County. *See* South Dakota
Buchannon, Roy, 143–146
bullies, 93–96, 112, 114
bullriding, 152–153
Bush, George H. W., xvii

C

camping out, 137, 140
Carlstrom Field, xiii
cars. *See* automobiles
cattle: broken leg and, 158–161; driving, 37–38; working, 152–153
Chicago, 121–122
childhood, xi–xii, 3–39
children, xiii, xxi, 167; advice to, xvi–xvii; childhood of, xxi–xxii; entertaining investors, xiv; photograph of, *131*; teaching gun safety, 30. *See also* names of individual children
church: First Baptist Church, 61, 167; parents and, xi
city kids, 13–14, 153
Clarksville, Texas, xiv, 135
coffins, 16–17
coin collection, 163–164
Colbath, Achsah Rebecca, 75–76
Colbath, Catherine, 76
Colbath, Edna Ruth. *See* Bentsen, Edna Colbath "Dolly"
Colbath, Edward, 76
colonel at Jefferson Barracks, 59–60
Colonel Reinhart's flying circus, 67
commissary, xiv–xv, 80–81
commission in Signal Corps, 69
confronting labor recruiters, 84–86
Connally, John, *128*
Consolidated American Life Insurance Company, xv–xvi
Consuelo (cook), xxi, xxii, 76–77
cooks, xxi, xxii, 76–77
county fair, 12–14

courtship, xii–xiii, 61, 62
cousins, Danish, 162–163. *See also* Bentsen, Magnus
credit cards, xiv–xv, 80–81

D

Dall mountain ram, 138–140
Danish heritage, 3–4, 53–54, 162–163
Dawson, Captain, 66–67
Depression, Great, xv, 121–122, *127*
doctors, 51–55, 161
Dohrn, Judge, 116–118
domestic violence, confronting, 93–96
driving: fatal accident, xviii; on ice, 31; in late life, xi; on sand, 81–82, 83; shot at, 87–88. *See also* automobiles; motorcycles
drowning, near, 36–37
duck hunting: at Black Slew (Oak Lake), 7–12; near drowning, 36–37; out of season, 135. *See also* hunting

E

education: enlistment and, 57; ground school at Princeton, 68–69; in South Dakota, 19–24, *41*
Edwards, Judge (attorney), 135
Elsa State Bank, xv
endorsing loans, 101–103
enlistment in Signal Corps, 56–60

F

family, xiii, 167; advising children, xvi–xvii; in Chicago, 121–122; labor disputes and, 87–89, 95–96, 109–110; philosophy on, xviii; photographs of, *42–44, 45, 124–131*. *See also* names of individual family members
family cemetery, 15–17
farm laborers. *See* labor relations; laborers
farmers, tenant, xxiv, 101–102
feuding, 75–77, 112, 144–146
fighting. *See* boxing; labor relations
financial success, 110–111
First Baptist Church, 61, 167
first date with Dolly, 62
First National Bank of Mission, xv, 103, 106–109
flying circus, 67
"Flying Wildcats" (198th Aero Squadron), 69
football, 19–22
Ford automobiles: enlistment and, 56, 58–59; honeymoon, xiii, 81–82, 83
fraud, insurance, 102
frontier medicine, 30

G

Gallagher, Jack, 6–7
gangsters, 121–122
Garcia, Juan, 109–110
Garner, John Nance, ix
Good Government League, 112
Good Neighbor Commission, xvi, 168
grandchildren, xxiv, *131*
graves, moving of, 15–17
Great Depression, xv, 121–122, *127*
great-grandchildren, *131*
grizzly bear encounter, 140
ground school, pilot, 68–69
gun safety, 14–15, 29–30, 154–156
guns: A. J. Aubrey shotgun, 7–12; accidental shootings, 23–24, 28–30; in airplanes, 67; American Legion celebration, xiii; bent rifle barrel, 33–34; gun control, xvii; labor disputes, 27–28, 87–89; loading own shotgun shells, 154–156; offered to Mullins, 114–115; at school, 22–24; target practice, xii; Yukon rifle, 139, 140

H

hair, unfashionable, 32–33
Henderson, Dr., 55
Heritage Hall of Honor, 168
Hickerson, Reverend, xxii
Hidalgo County, Texas, xviii, 90–91
hobos, xii, 6–7
Hoffa, Jimmy, 15–151, 148
honesty, xxii, 60
honeymoon, 81–84
honors and awards, 167–168
horses: motorcycle accident and, 49–50; in South Dakota, 5–6, 8, 14, 24–25, 29; in Yukon, 137
hunting: at Black Slew (Oak Lake), 7–12; geese, 147–148; near drowning, 36–37; out of season, 135; preference shooting, 14–15; on Rincón Ranch, *129*; with self-loaded shotgun shells, 154–156; in Yukon, 136–140. *See also* guns

I

ice skating, 31
immigration of family, xi, 3–4, 165–166
Indian Territory, 3, 15–16
Industrial Workers of the World (IWW), 25–28. *See also* Teamsters
infection, danger of, 54
injuries. *See* accidents
insurance, xv–xvi, 102, 168

171

investors: borrowing from, 100–101; liquor and, xxiii; recruiting, xii–xiv, xxii–xxiii
irrigation, 86–87, 112–118
IWW. *See* Industrial Workers of the World

J

jam, blackberry, 156–158
Jefferson Barracks, St. Louis, Mo., xii, 59–60
John (uncle), 17–18
Johnson, Lyndon B., *128*
José (Macrecio's son), 93, 96

K

Kiamachi Mountains, 143–146
knife attack, 98–99
Knud (Danish cousin), 162–163
Kymish Ranch, 135

L

labor relations: broken tractor shooting, 90–91; confronting recruiters, 84–86; family and, 87–89, 95–96, 109–110; irrigating neighbor's property, 86–89; unions and, 25–28, 148–151
laborers: credit cards for, xiv–xv, 80–81; union, 25–28
Lake Ponsett, 36–37
land: Bentsen State Park, xv; buying of, xviii; for children, xxiii–xxiv; clearing of, 80–81; love of, xv; partnership, xiv; property swapping, xiv; purchase of, xv, 100, 119–120; rising values, xv seeking investors for, xiii, xxii–xxiii; "three dollar land," 119–121; value of, 120–121, 165–166
Landry, Ray, xii, 61
Landry, Tommy, 61
leg, broken: by cow, 158–161; in motorcycle accident, xii, 51–52; rebreaking of, xii, 52–55
Lincoln Liberty Life Insurance Company, 168
liquor: investors and, xxiii; moonshine, 104–105; swearing off, xiii, 79
loans, endorsing, 101–103
loose-leaf notebooks, 63, 66–67
Lowry, David, *130*
Lowry, Susan Winn, xxiv, *130*
lullabies, Danish, 162–163
Lupe (cook), xxi, xxiii, 76–77, 87
Luz (servant), 76–77

M

Macrecio, 93–96
Marine Corps League Citation of Merit, 168
marksmanship, xii, xiii, 139–140, 147–148
Mayo, Charlie, 52, 54, 55

Mayo, William, 52, 54, 55
Mayo Brothers Clinic, xii, 52–55
McAllen family, xv
mechanic in World War I, 60, 64–67
medicine, frontier, 30
Menger Hotel, 82
Mexican workers, 80–81, 101–102. *See also* labor relations
Mexico: Good Neighbor Commission, xvi, 168; hunting in, 154–155; investors and, xxii–xxiii
Middleton, Mr. (of Chicago), 7, 11–12
military service: Minuteman award, xvi *129*, 168; Signal Corps, xii–xiii, *45*, 56–71; Texas State Guard, xvi, xxiii, 167
Minneapolis, Minnesota, xii, 56–57, 65–67
Minuteman award, xvi, *129*, 168
Mission, Texas, 167; American Legion celebration, 78–80; courtship, xii–xiii, 61, 62; first home with Dolly, 77–78; labor disputes, 84–89
Mississippi labor recruiters, 85–86
money: baby blue dress, 81–84; borrowing, 100–103; commissary and, 80–81; Dolly's inheritance, 75–76; philosophy on, xviii
moonshine, 104–105
Moose, Yukon hunting guide, 137–140
mortgages, 91–93, 101
motorcycles: accident, xii, 38, *43*, 49–55; racing, xii, 49–50. *See also* automobiles
mountains, 137, 138
mules, mortgaged, 91–93, 101
Mullins, Ernest, 112–118
mustangs, 24–25. *See also* horses

N

National Guard Association of Texas, xvi, *129*, 168
neighbors, 26, 86–87
1929 stock market crash, 103, 106–109
nurses, 52, 54–55
Nurses Home, 51–52

O

Oak Lake (Black Slew), 7–12
Ojo de Agua, 88–89
Oklahoma, 144–146
198th Aero Squadron "Flying Wildcats," 69

P

parents: as immigrants, xi, 165–166; move to Texas, xiii; in San Antonio, 121–122. *See also* Bentsen, Niels; Bentsen, Tena
partnership with Elmer, xiv, 103

172

patrón, Lloyd as, 75–122
Pedro (pony), 8, 14
Petersen, Anton, 3
Petersen, Emma, 4
Petersen, Hanne, 3, 15–17
Petersen, Laura, 4
Petersen, Miller, 4, 15–16, 17–18
Petersen, Tena. *See* Bentsen, Tena Petersen
pigs, 94
pilot, in World War I, xii–xiii, 68–69
pioneer, Lloyd as, 3–39
pistols: offered to Mullins, 114–115; in school, 22–24; union laborers and, 27–28. *See also* guns
pneumonia, fear of, 10
poems, xvii, 141–143
politics, xvii, 112–114, *128*
ponies. *See* horses
prairie fires, 4–5
pranks, 22–23, 62
prayer, xxiii
Princeton University, xiii, 68–69
Prohibition, 104–105

R

racing, xii, 49–50
Ramirez, Higinio, 91–93
Reidland, Ken, 161
Reinhart, Colonel, 67
Rhea, Charley, 114
riding, horseback: in South Dakota, 5–6, 24–25, 29; in Yukon, 137
rifles. *See* guns
Rincón Ranch, 160–161
Rio Grande Children's Home, 167
Rio Grande Valley, viii, ix, xii, xviii, 112–118
river crossing, 136–137

S

San Antonio, Texas: honeymoon, xiii, 81–84; visiting parents, 121–122; during WWI, 60
schools: class photo, *41*; football, 19–22; guns in, 22–24; pilot ground school, 68–69
sergeants, 59, 63–64
servants, xxi, xxii, xxiii, 77–78
Service, Robert W., 12
Shary, John H., xiii
Sharyland School, xxii, 113–114
sheep, 138–140
shells, 22–23, 154–156
sheriff and mortgaged mules, 91–93
Shivers, Allan, xvi
shooting: accidental, 23–24, 28–30; from airplanes, 67; American Legion celebration, 78–80; from cars, 154–156; employees and, 87–89, 90–91, 95–96; marksmanship, xii, xiii, 139–140, 147–148; preference shooting, 14–15
shotguns, 7–12, 154–155. *See also* guns
Sidse (Danish cousin), 162–163
Signal Corps, 167; enlistment, 56–60; mechanic, 60, 63–67; pilot, xii–xiii, *46*, 68–71. *See also* military service
Silver Beaver Award, 168
Sioux Falls, South Dakota, 57
Slick, Tom Sr. "Wildcatter," xv, 119–120
Smith, tenant farmer, xxiv
Smith family vs. Teamsters, 148–151
sobriety, xiii, 79
sod house, 165
songs, 38–39, 162–163
Sothebys Auction, 164
South Dakota, xi–xii, 3–39, 57
Stermer, Ed, 14–15
stock market, 76, 103, 106–109
stockholder notes, 106–108
storyteller, Lloyd as, viii, xxi, xxiv
strategy, boxing, 31–33
success, 110–111, 165–166
surgery, bone, 54

T

teachers, 19–20; and first wings, 70–71; football and, 20, 21
Teamsters, 148–151. *See also* Industrial Workers of the World (IWW)
tenant farmers, xxiv, 101–102
Texas A&M University award, 168
Texas Business Hall of Fame, 168
Texas Commerce Bank, 168
Texas Defense Guard battalion, xvi, xxiii, 167
Texas State Fair Heritage Hall of Honor, 168
Texas State Guard, xvi, xxiii, 167
Thanksgiving Day boxing match, 32–33
"three dollar land," 119–121
threshing machine, 17–18
tourniquet, 50–51
tractor, broken, 90–91
training manual, 63, 66–67
troubleshooter on the field, 64

U

unions, 25–28, 148–151

V

Valley Chamber of Commerce, 168
Valley Sportsman's Club, 168

Viking heritage, 53–54

W

wages: advanced to Paredes Ballí, 97–98; of Consuelo and Lupe, 77–78; credit cards and, xiv–xv, 80–81; as farm laborer, 6–7
water, in Yukon, 138
watermelons, 118–119
Western Union, 141–143
White, South Dakota, xi–xii, 38–39
Wichita Falls, 63–65
Wilson, Dick, 104–105, 106–108
Wimodasis Clubhouse, 113
wings, first, *46*, 70–71
Winn, Betty Bentsen (daughter): advertising Rio Grande Valley grapefruit, *125*; at Bentsen State Park, *130*; childhood of, xiv, xxii, xxiii; Dad's blackberry jam, 157; family photographs, *127*; on father, xxi–xxv; as landlord, xxiii–xxiv; mentioned, vii–viii, ix, xiii, 136, 162, 167
Winn, Dan, xxiv, *130*, 162
Winn, Dan Jr., xxiv, *130*
wolves, 29
work hours, 25–26
World War I, xii–xiii, *45*, 167; airplane mechanic, 63–67; enlisting, 56–60; first wings, *46*, 70–71; pilot ground school, 68–69
World War II, xvi, xxiii, *127*

Y

Yarborough, Ralph, xvii
Ybarra, Apolonio, 102
youth, 3–39
Yukon hunting trip, 136–140